JAPANESE KANJI MNEMONICS JLPT N3

JAPANESE KANJI MNEMONICS JLPT N3

Lindsay Jimenez

Dioxelis Lopez

2022

ACKNOWLEDGEMENTS

I can sincerely say that this third book was quite a bit of work, which I was not even expecting! However, I truly enjoyed making every kanji mnemonic in this book. I would also like to thank my supporters, my family, and the Japan Society of Fairfield County, in Connecticut, USA, for always being behind these efforts.

I truly hope you enjoy this book and that you get as much out of it as I did!

Book designed and written by Lindsay Jimenez

Cover design by Harold Jimenez

Formatting by Dioxelis Lopez

English editing by Pete Kuzmich

Kanji stroke diagrams are based on data from KanjiVG

Copyright © 2022 Japanese Kanji Mnemonics JLPT N3

All rights reserved

No part of this book may be reproduced in any form without written permission from the publisher.

Table of Contents

- HOW TO USE THIS BOOK 9
- SUMMARY OF JLPT N5 & N4 KANJI 10
- KANJI STROKE ORDER RULES 13
- **CHAPTER 1: ANIMALS** 15
  - 虫 INSECT 18
  - 貝 SHELLFISH 18
  - 羊 SHEEP 18
  - 馬 HORSE 20
  - 象 ELEPHANT 20
  - 牧 BREED, PASTURE 20
  - 羽 FEATHER 22
  - 巣 NEST, HIVE 22
  - 皮 SKIN, FUR 22
- **CHAPTER 2: FOOD** 23
  - 酒 ALCOHOL 26
  - 油 OIL 26
  - 氷 ICE 26
  - 麦 WHEAT 28
  - 梅 PLUM 28
  - 果 FRUIT, CARRY OUT 28
  - 豆 BEANS 30
  - 塩 SALT 30
  - 米 UNCOOKED RICE 30
- **CHAPTER 3: PEOPLE** 31
  - 孫 GRANDCHILD 34
  - 児 YOUNG CHILD 34
  - 童 JUVENILE, CHILD 34
  - 王 KING 36
  - 士 GENTLEMAN, SAMURAI 36
  - 夫 HUSBAND 36
  - 司 DIRECTOR, OFFICIAL 38
  - 副 ASSISTANT, AIDE 38
  - 臣 RETAINER, SUBJECT 38
  - 卒 GRADUATE, SOLDIER 40
  - 記 SCRIBE, NARRATIVE 40
  - 博 DR., COMMAND 40
  - 客 VISITOR, GUEST 42
- 君 YOU, RULER 42
- 老 OLD PERSON, GROW OLD 42
- 軍 ARMY 44
- 兵 SOLDIER 44
- 隊 SQUAD, CREW 44
- 係 PERSON IN CHARGE 46
- 治 REIGN, BE AT PEACE, HEAL, GOVERNMENT 46
- 官 BUREAUCRAT, THE GOVERNMENT 46
- **CHAPTER 4: BODY PARTS** 47
  - 胃 STOMACH 50
  - 腸 INTESTINES 50
  - 脈 VEIN 50
  - 鼻 NOSE 52
  - 歯 TOOTH 52
  - 身 BODY, ONESELF 52
  - 指 FINGER 54
  - 毛 HAIR, WOOL 54
  - 血 BLOOD 54
- **CHAPTER 5: NATURE** 55
  - 星 STAR 58
  - 景 SCENERY, VIEW 58
  - 原 FIELD 58
  - 波 WAVE 60
  - 湖 LAKE 60
  - 汽 STEAM, VAPOR 60
  - 流 CURRENT, FLOW 62
  - 湯 HOT WATER 62
  - 陽 SUNSHINE, POSITIVE 62
  - 芽 BUD, SPROUT 64
  - 葉 LEAF 64
  - 草 GRASS, WEED 64
  - 石 STONE 66
  - 岩 ROCK 66
  - 島 ISLAND 66
  - 岸 BEACH 68
  - 炭 CHARCOAL 68
  - 畑 FIELD, FARM 68
- 熱 HEAT, TEMPERATURE 70
- 陸 LAND 70
- 毒 POISON 70
- 農 AGRICULTURE, FARMERS 72
- 根 ROOT 72
- 松 PINE TREE 72
- 粉 POWDER 74
- 種 SEED 74
- 季 SEASON 74
- 候 CLIMATE, SEASON 76
- 節 SEASON, TUNE 76
- 竹 BAMBOO 76
- 雲 CLOUD 78
- 雪 SNOW 78
- 鉄 IRON 78
- **CHAPTER 6: OBJECTS** 79
  - 玉 JEWEL, BALL 82
  - 球 SPHERE 82
  - 柱 PILLAR, COLUMN 82
  - 機 MACHINE, DEVICE, LOOM 84
  - 械 MACHINE, GADGET 84
  - 材 LUMBER, LOG, TIMBER, MATERIAL 84
  - 札 TOKEN, BANKNOTE 86
  - 標 SIGNPOST, LABEL 86
  - 票 BALLOT, TICKET 86
  - 帯 SASH, ZONE 88
  - 席 SEAT 88
  - 帳 CURTAIN, NOTEBOOK 88
  - 糸 YARN, THREAD 90
  - 絵 PAINTING 90
  - 束 BUNDLE, BUNCH 90
  - 船 SHIP 92
  - 器 VESSEL 92
  - 荷 BAGAGGE, LOAD 92
  - 賞 PRIZE 94
  - 貨 GOODS, FREIGHT 94
  - 管 PIPE 94

筆 WRITING BRUSH 96	科 DEPARTMENT, COURSE, SECTION 122	害 HARM, INJURY 150
箱 BOX, CHEST 96	丁 STREET, WARD 124	関 CONNECTION, GATEWAY 150
笛 FLUTE 96	寺 TEMPLE 124	**CHAPTER 9: FEELINGS** 151
矢 ARROW 98	里 VILLAGE 124	愛 LOVE, AFFECTION 154
弓 BOW 98	**CHAPTER 8: ABSTRACT** 125	恋 ROMANCE, IN LOVE 154
刀 SWORD 98	神 GODS, MIND 128	想 CONCEPT, THINK, THOUGHT 154
具 TOOL, UTENSIL 100	福 BLESSING, WEALTH 128	念 WISH, DESIRE 156
旗 FLAG 100	礼 CEREMONY, BOW 128	感 EMOTION, FEELING 156
輪 WHEEL 100	貯 SAVINGS, STORE 130	信 FAITH, TRUST 156
型 MOLD 102	相 MUTUAL, EACH OTHER 130	功 ACHIEVEMENT, MERITS 158
板 BOARD, PLANK 102	観 OUTLOOK, APPEARANCE 130	勇 COURAGE, BRAVERY 158
印 SEAL 102	組 CLASS, CREW, SET 132	希 HOPE, RARE 158
灯 LAMP 104	給 SALARY, WAGE 132	幸 HAPPINESS, BLESSING 160
皿 DISH, PLATE 104	級 CLASS, RANK 132	栄 FLOURISH, PROSPERITY 160
衣 CLOTHES 104	利 PROFIT, ADVANTAGE 134	和 HARMONY, PEACE 160
鏡 MIRROR 106	列 FILE, ROW 134	敗 FAILURE, DEFEAT 162
面 MASK, FACE 106	残 REMAINS, LEFTOVER 134	**CHAPTER 10: ADJECTIVES** 163
角 ANGLE, CORNER, HORN 106	戦 WAR, BATTLE, MATCH 136	丸 ROUND, CURL UP 166
CHAPTER 7: PLACES 107	式 CEREMONY, SYSTEM 136	才 GENIUS, YEARS OLD 166
庫 WAREHOUSE, DEPOSITORY 110	差 DISTICTION, DIFFERENCE 136	良 GOOD, PLEASING 166
庭 COURTYARD, GARDEN 110	由 A REASON 138	悲 GRIEVE, SAD 168
府 GOVERNMENT OFFICE, PREFECTURE 110	位 RANK, GRADE, THRONE 138	必 CERTAIN, INEVITABLE 168
園 GARDEN, PLANTATION 112	氏 SURNAME, CLAN 138	変 STRANGE, UNUSUAL 168
坂 SLOPE 112	役 DUTY, WAR 140	最 MOST, EXTREME 170
街 TOWN 112	徒 ON FOOT, FUTILITY 140	昭 SHINING, BRIGHT 170
戸 DOOR 114	欠 LACK, GAP 140	温 WARM 170
局 BUREAU, OFFICE 114	順 OBEY, ORDER, DOCILITY 142	浅 SHALLOW, SUPERFICIAL 172
橋 BRIDGE 114	類 SORT, KIND 142	深 DEEP, INTENSIFY 172
倉 STOREHOUSE 116	共 TOGETHER, BOTH 142	満 FULL, SATISFY 172
宮 SHRINE, PALACE 116	令 ORDER, LAW 144	清 PURE, PURIFY 174
宿 LODGING, INN 116	命 FATE, LIFE 144	静 QUIET 174
公 PUBLIC 118	的 MARK, TARGET 144	冷 COLD, CHILL 174
谷 VALLEY 118	協 COOPERATION 146	速 QUICK, FAST 176
路 PATH, ROUTE 118	芸 TECHNIQUE, ART 146	苦 SUFFERING, BITTER 176
郡 DISTRICT 120	形 SHAPE, FORM 146	完 PERFECT, COMPLETION 176
部 SECTION, BUREAU 120	量 QUANTITY, MEASURE, AMOUNT 148	単 SIMPLE, SINGLE 178
階 STAIRS 120	予 BEFOREHAND, MYSELF 148	平 EVEN, PEACE 178
港 HARBOR, PORT 122	祭 RITUAL, CELEBRATE 148	美 BEAUTY, BEAUTIFUL 178
州 SANDBANK, STATE 122	実 REALITY, TRUTH 150	細 GET THIN, NARROW, PRECISE 180

緑 GREEN 180	談 DISCUSS, TALK 208	折 FOLD, BREAK, FRACTURE 238
黄 YELLOW 180	各 EACH, EVERY 210	打 STRIKE, HIT 238
等 ETC., EQUAL, CLASS 182	願 PETITION, REQUEST, HOPE 210	投 THROW, ABANDON 238
努 TOIL, DILIGENT 182	章 BADGE, CHAPTER, COMPOSITION .. 210	固 HARDEN, CURDLE 240
全 WHOLE, ENTIRE 182	例 EXAMPLE 212	登 ASCEND, CLIMB UP 240
健 HEALTHY, STRENGTH 184	他 OTHERS, ANOTHER 212	喜 REJOICE, TAKE PLEASURE IN 240
康 EASE, PEACE 184	典 CODE, CEREMONY, LAW 212	航 NAVIGATE, SAIL 242
直 STRAIGHT, HONESTY 184	無 NOTHINGNESS, NONE, NOT 214	商 MAKE A DEAL, MERCHANT 242
CHAPTER 11: POSITION + TIME 185	然 SORT OF THING, IF SO 214	停 HALT, STOPPING 242
央 CENTER, MIDDLE 188	録 RECORD 214	化 CHANGE, INFLUENCE 244
仲 GO-BETWEEN, RELATIONSHIP 188	案 PLAN, EXPECTATION 216	伝 TRANSMIT, REPORT 244
側 SIDE, OPPOSE 188	法 METHOD, LAW, RULE 216	付 ATTACH, ADHERE 244
内 INSIDE, WITHIN 190	約 PROMISE, APPROXIMATELY 216	整 ORGANIZE, ARRANGING 246
周 CIRCUMFERENCE, LAP 190	**CHAPTER 13: SPEECH** 217	散 SCATTER, DISPERSE 246
表 SURFACE, TABLE 190	号 NUMBER, ITEM, TITLE 220	救 SAVE, HELP 246
末 END 192	第 No., RESIDENCE 220	放 SET FREE, EMIT 248
横 SIDEWAYS, HORIZONTAL 192	番 TURN, NUMBER IN A SERIES 220	改 REFORMATION, MODIFY 248
秒 SECOND 192	数 NUMBER, FIGURES 222	包 WRAP, PACK UP 248
反 AGAINST, ANTI- 194	算 CALCULATE, NUMBER, PROBABILITY .. 222	遊 PLAY 250
歴 CURRICULUM, PASSAGE OF TIME .. 194	点 SPOT, MARK 222	追 CHASE, FOLLOW 250
史 HISTORY, CHRONICLE 194	両 BOTH 224	選 ELECT, CHOOSE 250
次 NEXT, ORDER 196	倍 DOUBLE, TIMES 224	連 TAKE ALONG, JOIN 252
辺 BORDER, VICINITY 196	径 DIAMETER, PATH 224	返 RETURN, REPAY 252
対 OPPOSITE, COMPARE 196	兆 TRILLION, OMEN 226	達 ATTAIN, REACH, PLURAL SUFFIX ... 252
昔 ONCE UPON A TIME 198	億 HUNDRED MILLION 226	辞 RESIGN, WORD 254
昨 YESTERDAY, PREVIOUS 198	積 VOLUME, PRODUCT 226	曲 MUSIC, BEND 254
期 PERIOD, TIME 198	**CHAPTER 14: VERBS PART I** 227	覚 MEMORIZE, REMEMBER 254
囲 SURROUND, ENCLOSURE 200	決 DECIDE, AGREE UPON 230	労 LABOR, TROUBLE 256
底 BOTTOM, SOLE 200	落 FALL, DROP 230	加 ADD, INCREASE 256
紀 CHRONICLE, HISTORY 200	消 EXTINGUISH, TURN OFF 230	助 HELP, RESCUE 256
CHAPTER 12: SPEECH 201	浴 BATHE, BE FAVORED WITH 232	**CHAPTER 15: VERBS PART II** 257
未 NOT YET, STILL 204	泳 SWIM 232	失 LOSE, ERROR 260
様 WAY, POLITE SUFFIX 204	漁 FISHING, FISHERY 232	求 REQUEST, WANT 260
極 VERY, POLES, SETTLEMENT 204	泣 CRY, WEEP 234	笑 LAUGH 260
課 CHAPTER, SECTION 206	活 LIVELY, RESUSCITATION, LIVING .. 234	察 GUESS, JUDGE 262
議 DELIVERATION, DEBATE 206	拾 PICK UP, GATHER 234	守 GUARD, PROTECT 262
詩 POETRY 206	当 HIT, APPROPRIATE 236	定 DETERMINE, ESTABLISH 262
調 TUNE, HARMONIZE, PREPARE 208	争 CONTEND, DISPUTE 236	飛 FLY, SCATTER 264
訓 INSTRUCTION, EXPLANATION 208	挙 RAISE, PLAN, PROJECT 236	要 NEED, MAIN POINT 264

養 FOSTER, BRING UP 264
息 BREATH 266
刷 PRINT, BRUSH..................................... 266
初 FIRST TIME, BEGINNING, START 266
成 TURN INTO, BECOME 268
配 DISTRIBUTE, EXCILE 268
昭 ILLUMINATE, SHINE............................ 268
晴 CLEAR UP... 270
唱 CHANT, RECITE 270
得 GAIN, EARN, PROFIT 270
委 COMMITTEE, ENTRUST TO 272
交 CROSS, MIXING 272

申 HAVE THE HONOR TO, SAY................272
鳴 CHIRP, BARK, CRY 274
向 YONDER, FACING, BEYOND 274
告 REVELATION, TELL, INFORM................274
競 COMPETE WITH, CONTEST, RACE.......276
祝 CELEBRATE, CONGRATULATE 276
焼 BAKE, BURNING 276
殺 KILL, MURDER 278
取 TAKE, FETCH..278
受 ACCEPT, UNDERGO 278
省 FOCUS, GOVERNMENT MINISTRY 280
植 PLANT...280

置 PLACEMENT, PUT, LEAVE BEHIND.....280
育 BRING UP, RAISE 282
望 AMBITION, HOPE, DESIRE 282
勝 VICTORY, WIN, EXCEL.........................282
負 DEFEAT, ASSUME A RESPONSIBILITY.284
費 EXPENSE, SPEND, WASTE 284
参 VISIT, GOING, COMING 284
練 PRACTICE, POLISH 286
続 CONTINUE, SERIES 286
結 TIE, BIND, FASTEN 286
INDEX...288

HOW TO USE THIS BOOK

The main goal of this book is to help those who are studying Japanese as a second language. For this reason, the book is centered on a specific Japanese Language Proficiency Test (JLPT) level. This third book, of the Japanese Kanji Mnemonics Series, focuses on the next 361 Japanese characters (kanji) found on the N3 level test and it assumes the reader has knowledge of the two Japanese alphabets (Hiragana and Katakana) as well as the 103 kanji required for the JLPT N5 and the 181 for the JLPT N4. In order to start using this book, please follow the following steps:

1. THE FRONT PAGE:
   a. <u>Flashcard Style</u>: The book is recommended to be used as flashcards. Therefore, the student will find the kanji mnemonic on the front page and the kanji information on the other side. Each front page contains a total of 3 kanji, which are related based on similarities such as radicals, same meanings, synonyms or antonyms.
   b. <u>Mnemonic</u>: Whenever possible, the drawings have been made to match the characters' radicals, elements, and history as much as possible. In the cases where this was not possible, this book tries to make it easy to remember. Some notes on etymology have also been included for clarification.

2. THE REVERSE PAGE:
   a. <u>Common Meaning(s)</u>: The student will find the meanings that are most appropriate for the N3 level.
   b. <u>Sentence</u>: A sentence to help remember the kanji better and that also creates a story that can be used as a mnemonic device. Each sentence was formed by breaking down the kanji into different elements for easy memorization. The elements can be radicals, components, kanji, or hanzi.
   c. <u>Stroke Order</u>: The order in which the kanji must be written.
   d. <u>Writing Exercise</u>: The student will have the opportunity to write the kanji in this section of the book for extra practice.
   e. <u>ON and Kun readings</u>: These serve as a guide for the student to only focus on learning and practicing the readings that will be required in the exam. Note: When a particular reading does not fall in either category, it will be noted as *ODD*
   f. <u>Examples</u>: In this section of the book, you will find the following:
      - Vocabulary: The words chosen for each kanji in this book are words relevant to the JLPT N3. This is to give the student the opportunity to practice vocabulary found in the exam.
      - Furigana: All words contain their corresponding furigana on top of each kanji.
   g. <u>Similar Kanji</u>: In this box the student will find kanji that is similar to the one they are learning and that the student can get easily confused with.

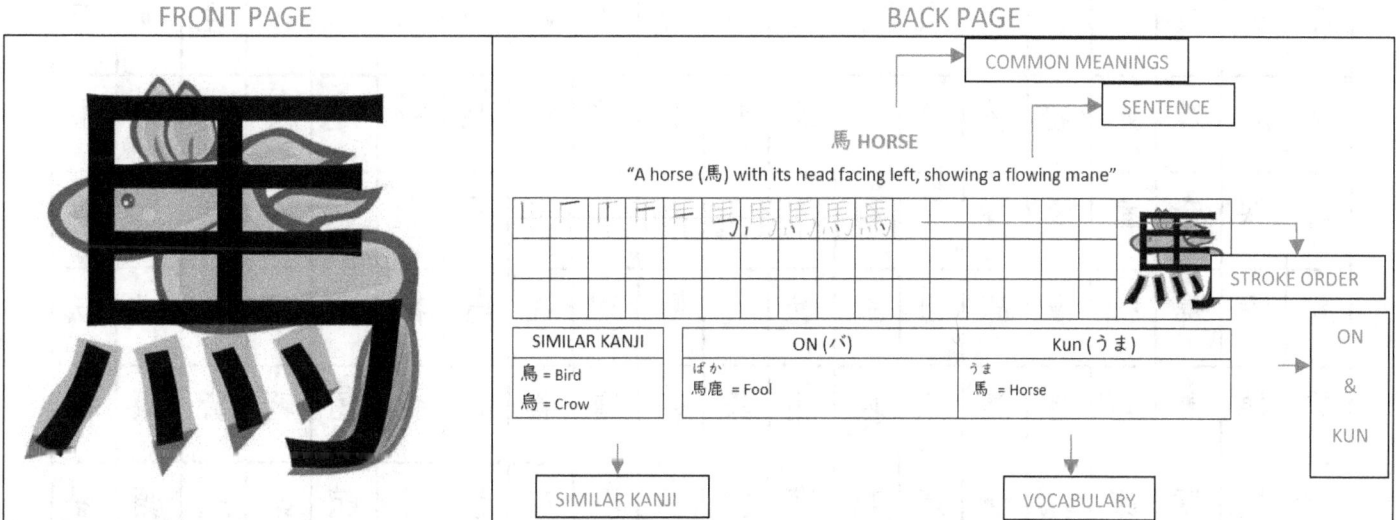

3. This book is not meant to be used on its own. It is highly recommended that the student also uses reading comprehension materials, such a fairy tales or books, as seeing the different kanji in actual sentences will reinforce what was learned in this book.

SUMMARY OF JLPT N5 & N4 KANJI

JLPT N5 KANJI

山	川	土	日	月	雨	水	木	天	火	本	魚	気	花	国	金	空	電	人	子
女	友	父	母	男	口	耳	目	足	手	社	車	店	校	道	駅	名	円	大	小
少	白	古	多	安	長	高	新	上	下	中	外	先	後	前	右	左	北	西	東
南	分	今	半	年	毎	何	時	週	間	午	一	二	三	四	五	六	七	八	九
十	百	千	万	入	出	生	立	会	行	休	見	言	来	学	食	買	飲	語	聞
読	書	話																	

JLPT N4 KANJI

カ	工	タ	方	不	区	心	文	元	引	止	切	太	牛	犬	民	市	代	田	主
用	以	世	正	台	広	仕	去	写	冬	兄	同	自	地	合	回	考	死	有	早
好	字	光	色	池	肉	体	作	近	売	別	私	村	住	町	究	声	低	医	図
赤	走	弟	事	者	明	京	画	知	物	使	所	始	英	味	門	夜	注	歩	青
林	服	妹	姉	発	首	度	持	思	県	界	重	海	品	計	建	急	送	研	乗
待	映	音	室	風	春	屋	秋	便	洋	昼	茶	洗	員	通	家	院	特	真	料
起	病	帰	紙	夏	旅	借	弱	勉	問	動	理	強	野	都	進	産	教	終	転
族	悪	黒	習	堂	鳥	菜	場	開	集	朝	運	着	答	森	短	軽	貸	飯	暑
寒	業	意	楽	試	働	遠	暗	漢	説	銀	歌	質	親	頭	館	薬	題	顔	曜
験																			

ELEMENTS & RADICALS

STROKE	ELEMENT	MEANING
1	乚	Bent
2	冫	Ice, two
2	又	Hand
2	ナ	Hand
2	亻	Person
2	人	Person
2	厶	I, myself
2	十	Ten
2	儿	Legs
2	冂	Enclosure
2	力	Strength
2	勹	Bent person
2	冖	Cover
2	刀	Sword, knife
2	刂	Sword, knife
2	匕	Spoon, ladle
2	厂	Cliff
2	卩	Kneel down
2	八	Divide
3	大	Big
3	寸	Measurement
3	艹	Plant, grass
3	辶	Road
3	彡	Hair, bright
3	广	Tent
3	夂	Feet
3	氵	Water, liquid
3	土	Soil, ground
3	士	Man, samurai
3	小	Small
3	弋	Spike
3	兀	Table
3	女	Woman
3	弓	Bow
3	宀	Roof, house
3	子	Child
3	阝	Hill
3	阝	City
3	工	Work, craft
3	巾	Cloth, scroll
3	口	Mouth, opening
3	囗	Enclosure
3	己	Straighten up
3	彳	Road
3	尸	Awning, corpse
3	也	To be
3	廾	Hands
3	川	River
3	山	Mountain
3	干	To dry
3	彐	Hand
3	臣	Hand
3	扌	Hands
3	亼	Roof
3	勺	Spoon
4	耂	Old
4	宀	Cave
4	中	Middle
4	毛	Hair
4	井	Well
4	犬	Dog
4	斗	Dipper, ladle
4	歹	Death
4	开	Two poles
4	云	Cloud
4	攵	Hit, whip
4	欠	To lack
4	爫	Hand
4	氏	Family, clan
4	方	Direction
4	尹	Govern
4	文	Literature, letters
4	夭	Young man
4	厶	Child
4	亢	High
4	殳	Tool
4	日	Day, sun
4	爻	Cross
4	灬	Fire
4	止	To stop
4	月	Moon
4	戈	Halberd
4	月	Flesh, body
4	火	Fire
4	木	Tree
4	丼	Flood, plant
4	牛	Cow
4	生	Cow
4	心	Heart
4	水	Water
4	韦	Plants
4	斤	Axe
4	气	Air
4	礻	Altar
5	且	Ancestor
5	合	Along
5	申	Lighting, to say
5	田	Rice field
5	生	Life
5	甲	Shield
5	乍	Create
5	癶	Footsteps
5	罒	Net
5	弗	Dollar
5	皿	Chalice, dish
5	白	White
5	王	King
5	矢	Arrow
5	立	To stand
5	石	Stone
5	由	Gourd
5	目	Eye
5	衣	Clothing
5	禾	Grain
5	甘	Sweet
5	示	Altar
5	戋	Halberd

6	羊	Sheep	6	襾	Covering	8	隹	Small bird
6	队	Flag pole	7	呂	Rooms	8	尚	High status
6	糸	Yarn, Thread	7	走	To run	8	雨	Rain
6	虫	Insect	7	車	Car, cart	8	長	Long
6	自	Stacks	7	豆	Bean	8	音	Split
6	舟	Boat	7	豕	Pig	8	其	Basket
6	米	Rice	7	辛	Bitter, tattooing needle	8	录	Green
6	囟	Brain	7	貝	Shell, money	8	門	Gate
6	聿	Brush	7	酉	Drinking vessel	9	畐	Container
6	羽	Feather	7	豆	Beans	9	昜	Sun rays
6	舌	Tongue	7	里	Village	9	食	Food
6	⺮	Bamboo	7	系	Lineage	9	頁	Head
6	艮	Good	7	言	Speech, word	10	馬	Horse
6	自	Self	7	辰	Garden fork	11	魚	Fish
6	丝	Yarn	8	金	Gold, metal	11	鳥	Bird
6	羊	Sheep	8	食	Food			

KANJI STROKE ORDER RULES

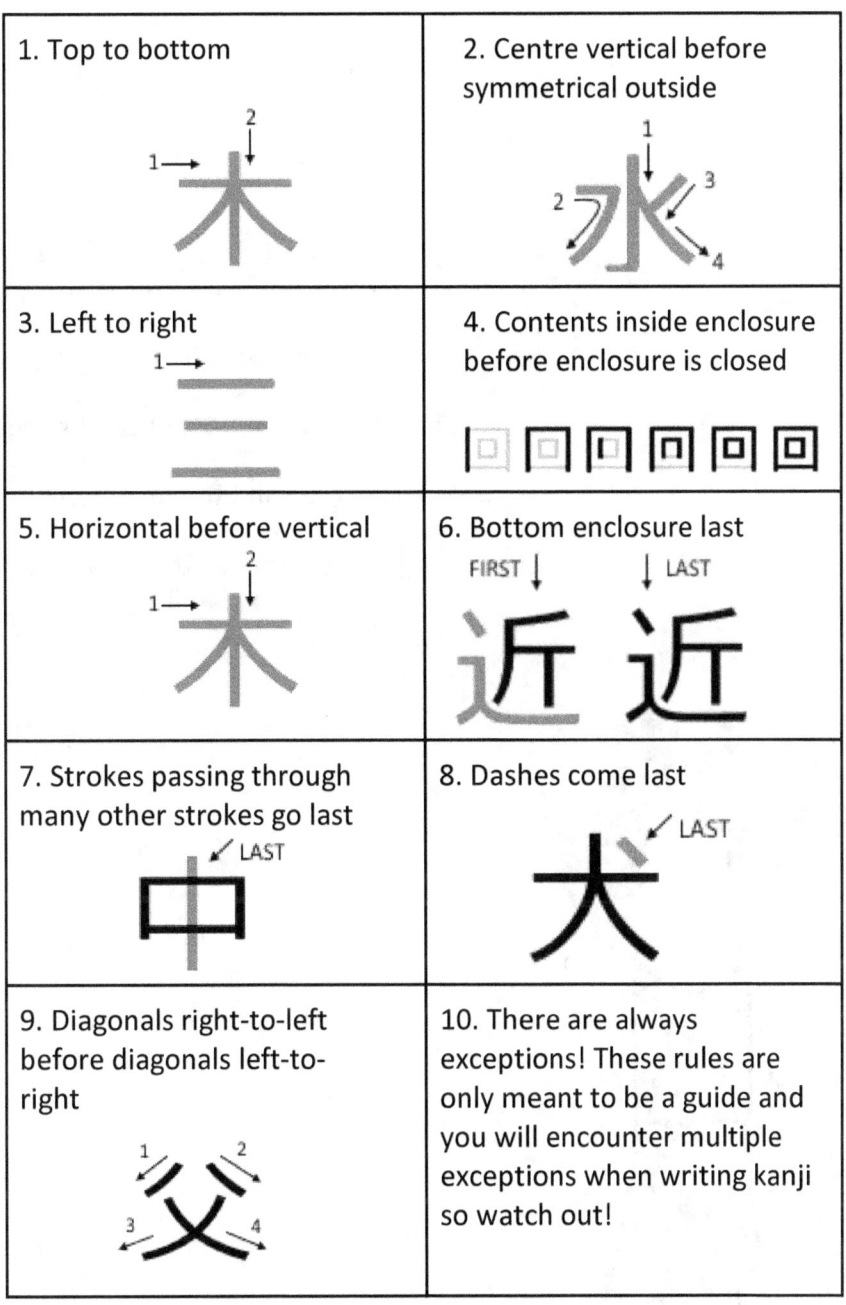

WHEN YOU LEARN KANJI:

1. Practice the stroke order

2. Practice the components/elements

3. Keep in mind the mnemonics

4. Read sentences that have the new kanji

CHAPTER 1: ANIMALS

虫	貝	羊
1	2	3
馬	象	牧
4	5	6
羽	巢	皮
7	8	9

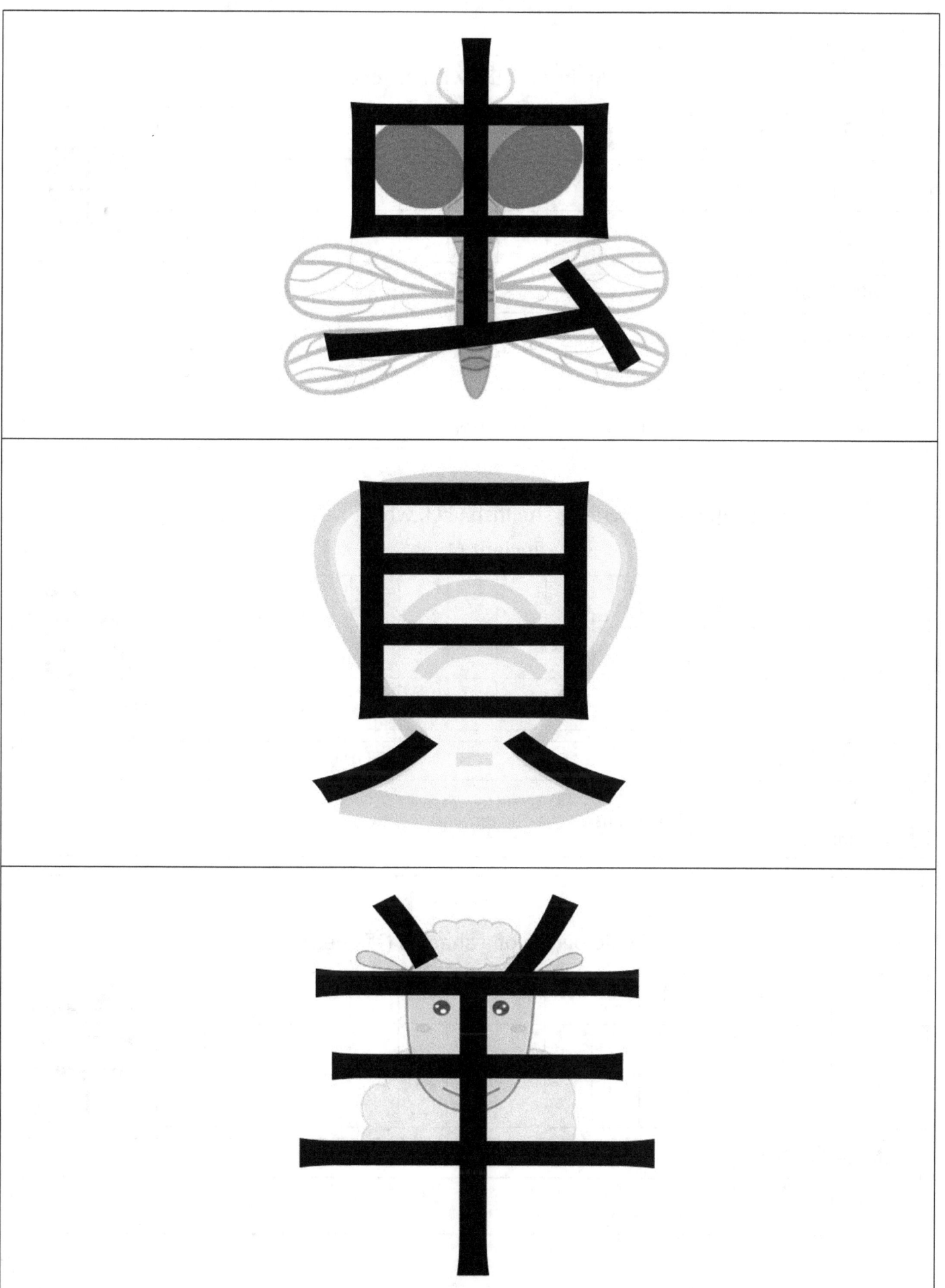

虫 INSECT

"An insect (虫) with big eyes"

SIMILAR KANJI	Kun (むし)	
中 = Inside 独 = Single	むし 虫 = Insect, bug	むしば 虫歯 = Cavity, tooth decay

*This kanji originally represented a venomous snake. It eventually took the meaning of insect.

貝 SHELLFISH

"The shape of a cowrie or shellfish (貝), which was used as money in ancient China"

SIMILAR KANJI	Kun (かい)
具 = Tool 員 = Employee	かい 貝 = Shellfish

羊 SHEEP

"A pictogram of a sheep's (羊) head"

SIMILAR KANJI	Kun (ひつじ)
洋 = Ocean	ひつじ 羊 = Sheep

馬

象

牧

馬 HORSE

"A horse (馬) with its head facing left, showing a flowing mane"

SIMILAR KANJI	ON (バ)	Kun (うま)
鳥 = Bird 烏 = Crow	ばか 馬鹿 = Fool	うま 馬 = Horse

象 ELEPHANT

"The trunk, the head, and the body of an elephant (象)"

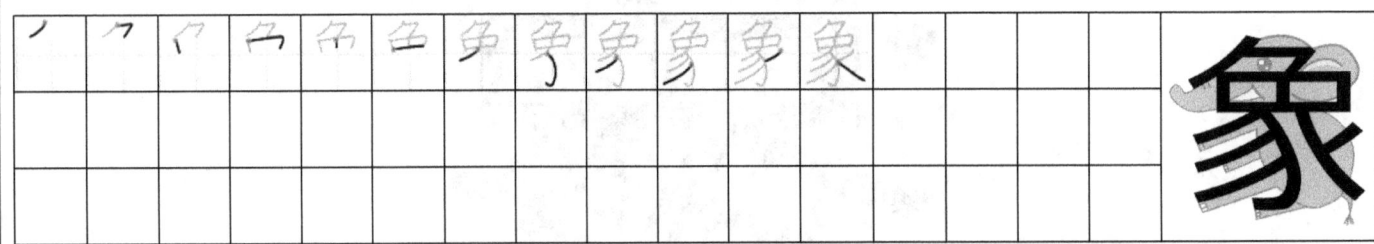

SIMILAR KANJI	ON (ゾウ、ショウ)	
像 = Image, statue	ぞう 象 = Elephant げんしょう 現 象 = Phenomenon	いんしょう 印 象 = Impression たいしょう 対 象 = Target

牧 BREED, PASTURE

"Use the whip (攵) to guide the cows (牛) to pasture (牧)"

SIMILAR KANJI	ON (ボク)
牲 = Animal sacrifice	ぼくちく 牧 畜 = Livestock farming

羽 FEATHER

"It looks like a bird's feathers (羽)"

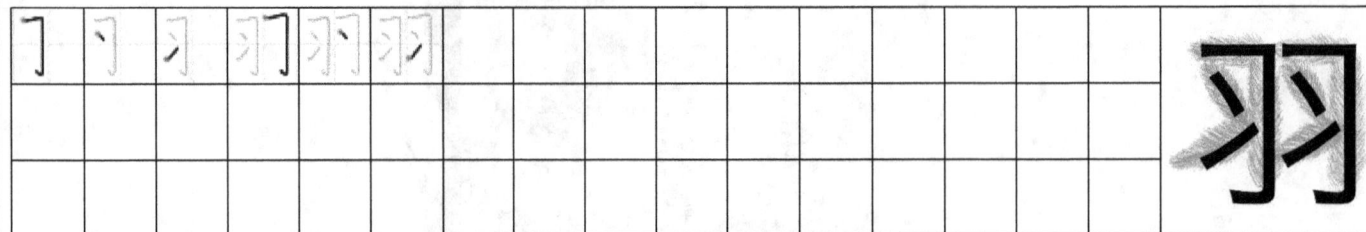

SIMILAR KANJI	Kun (はね)
弱 = Weak	はね 羽 = Feather

巣 NEST, HIVE

"The small (小) birds made a nest (巣) on the tree (木) bearing fruits (果)"

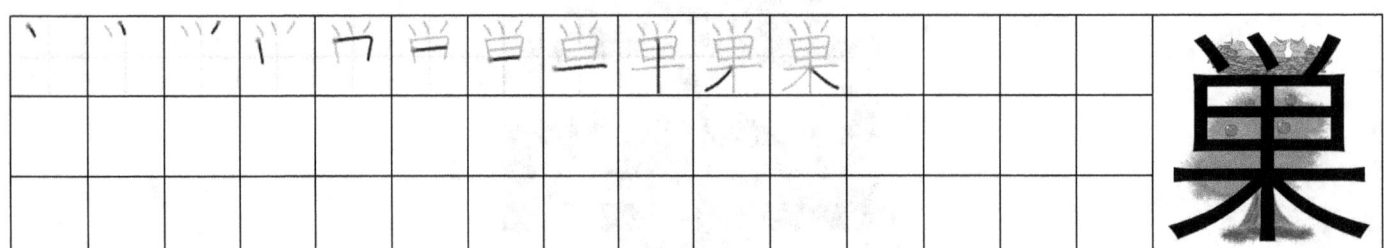

SIMILAR KANJI	Kun (す)
単 = Simple 果 = Fruit	す 巣 = Nest

皮 SKIN, FUR

"A hand (又) stripping the fur (皮) from an animal"

SIMILAR KANJI	Kun (かわ)	
彼 = He 波 = Waves	かわ 皮 = Skin, fur	けがわ 毛皮 = Fur, skin, pelt

CHAPTER 2: FOOD

酒	油	冰
10	11	12
麦	梅	果
13	14	15
豆	塩	米
16	17	18

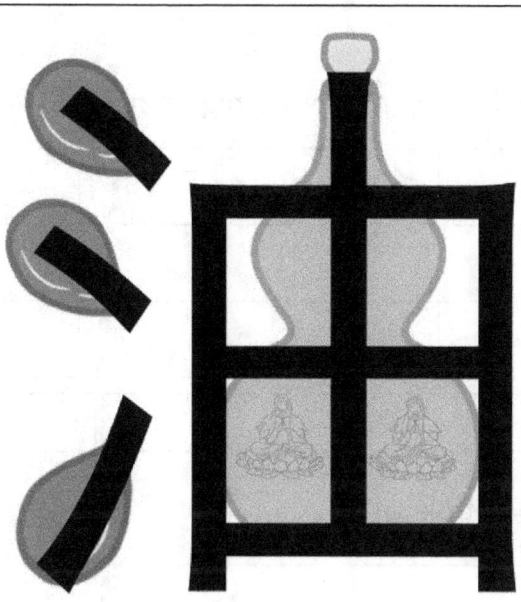

酒 ALCOHOL

"The liquid (氵) inside the drinking vessel (酉) is alcohol (酒)"

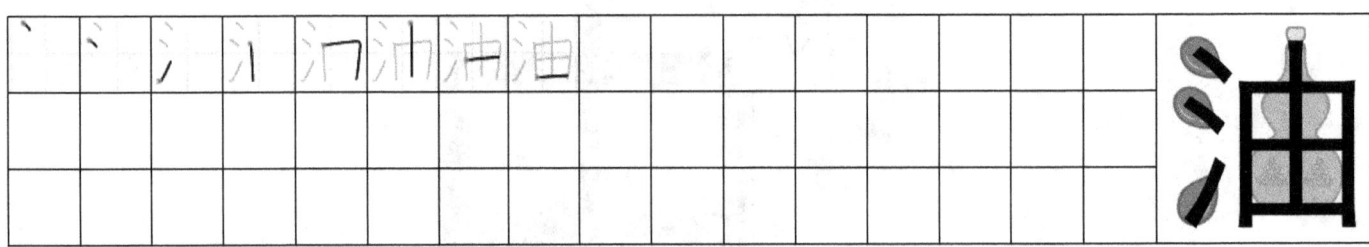

SIMILAR KANJI	Kun (さけ)	
酌 = Serving sake	お酒 (さけ) = Alcohol, sake	酒 (さけ) = Alcohol, sake

油 OIL

"The liquid (氵) inside the big gourd (由) is oil (油)"

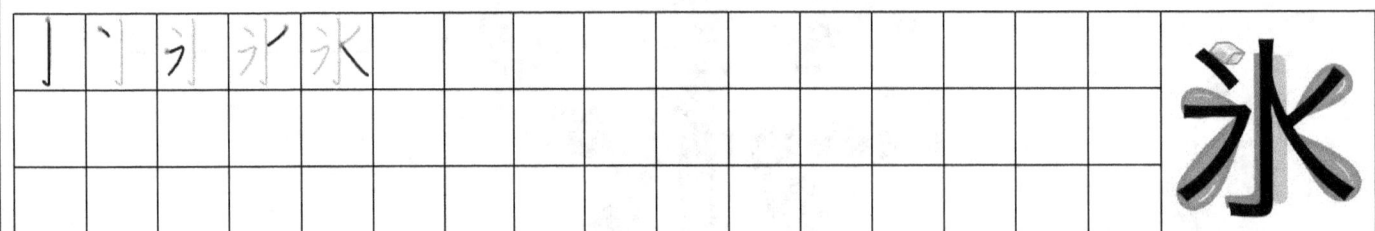

SIMILAR KANJI	ON (ユ)	Kun (あぶら)
抽 = Pluck, pull 由 = A reason	石油 (せきゆ) = Petroleum	油 (あぶら) = Oil

氷 ICE

"You can turn water (水) into ice (氷)"

SIMILAR KANJI	ON (ひょう)	Kun (こおり)
永 = Eternity 水 = Water	氷河 (ひょうが) = Glacier	氷 (こおり) = Ice

麦

梅

果

麦 WHEAT

"The farmer put his best foot (夂) forward easy for the spring gathering of wheat (麦) plants (龶)"

SIMILAR KANJI	Kun (むぎ)
素 = Elementary 表 = Surface	こむぎ 小麦 = Wheat

梅 PLUM

"Every (毎) year, when plum (梅) trees (木) blossom, it means the start of spring"

SIMILAR KANJI	ON (バイ)	Kun (うめ)	ODD (つ)
海 = Sea 毎 = Every	ばいう 梅雨 = Rainy season	うめ 梅 = Japanese plum	つゆ 梅雨 = Rainy season

果 FRUIT, CARRY OUT

"A tree (木) with big fruits (果) on the top"

SIMILAR KANJI	ON (カ)	ODD (くだ)
単 = Simple 早 = Early	こうか 効果 = Efficacy けっか 結果 = Result	くだもの 果物 = Fruit

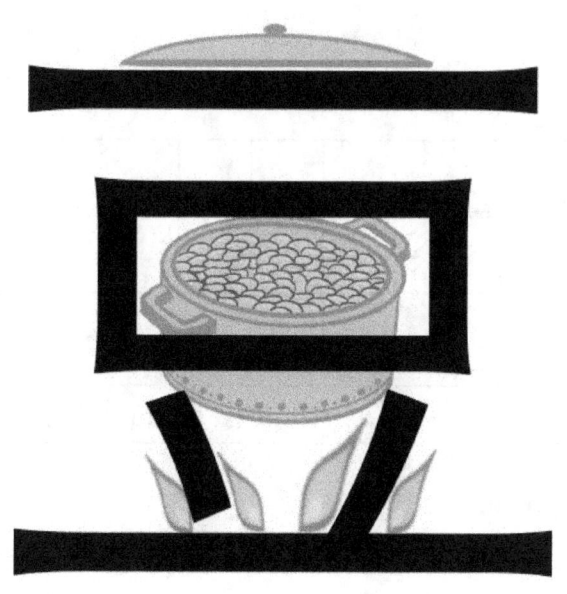

豆 BEANS
"Cooking a bowl of beans (豆)"

SIMILAR KANJI	Kun (まめ)
痘 = Smallpox 登 = Ascend	まめ 豆 = Beans

塩 SALT
"The person (亻) dropped salt (塩) on the ground (土) and puts it back on a dish (皿)"

SIMILAR KANJI	Kun (しお)
温 = Warm	しお 塩 = Salt

米 UNCOOKED RICE
"A rice (米) plant and its grains"

SIMILAR KANJI	ON (マイ)	Kun (こめ)
来 = Come 水 = Water	しんまい 新米 = New rice	こめ 米 = Uncooked rice

CHAPTER 3: PEOPLE

孫	児	童	王	士	夫
19	20	21	22	23	24
司	副	臣	卒	記	博
25	26	27	28	29	30
客	君	老	軍	兵	隊
31	32	33	34	35	36
係	治	官			
37	38	39			

孫

児

童

孫 GRANDCHILD

"There is one more child (子)... yes, a grandchild (孫) in our lineage (系)"

SIMILAR KANJI	ON (ソン)	Kun (まご)
系 = Lineage 係 = Person in charge	しそん 子孫 = Offspring	まご 孫 = Grandchild

児 YOUNG CHILD

"A young child (児) crawling under the sun (日)"

SIMILAR KANJI	ON (ジ)	
旧 = Old times	ようじ 幼児 = Toddler, young child	じどう 児童 = Juvenile, children

*The original kanji was 兒 which was a baby whose fontanel had not closed yet.

童 JUVENILE, CHILD

"The juveniles (童) in the village (里) play by standing (立) on one foot"

SIMILAR KANJI	ON (ドウ)	Kun (わらべ)
量 = Quantity 章 = Chapter	じどう 児童 = Juvenile, children	わらべ 童 = Child

*The original kanji was long and complex, and it meant prisoner/slave. Someone considered ignorant, like a prisoner, was compared to a child.

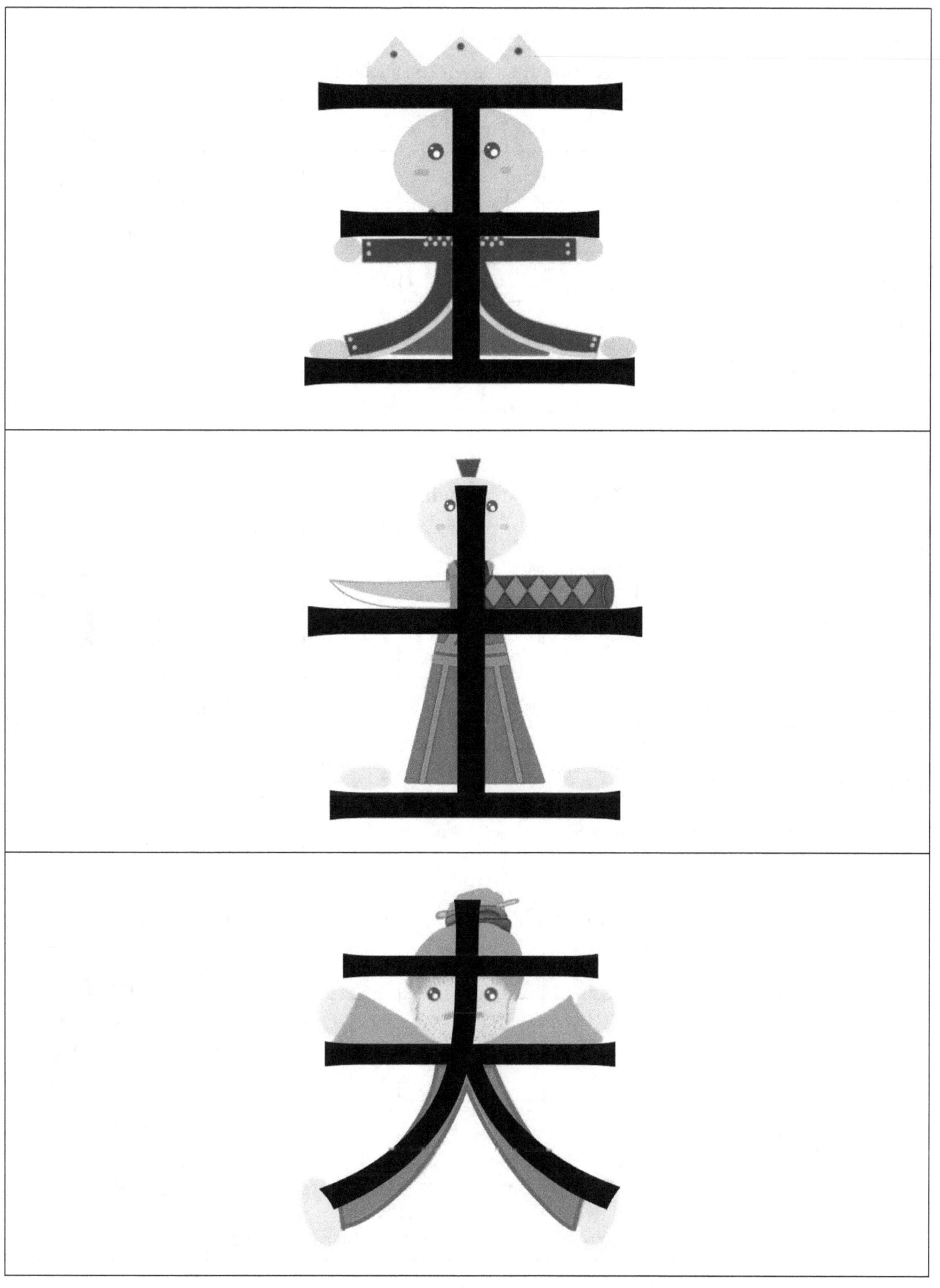

王 KING

"A king (王) wearing his crown to symbolize his power"

SIMILAR KANJI	ON (オウ)		
玉 = Ball 主 = Chief	おう 王 = King, monarch	おうじ 王子 = Prince	おうさま 王様 = King

*The original kanji consisted of an ornamental axe of a ruler that signified power.

士 GENTLEMAN, SAMURAI

"A samurai (士) holding a sword"

SIMILAR KANJI	ON (シ)	ODD (せ)
土 = Earth 仕 = Attend	べんごし 弁護士 = Lawyer	はかせ 博士 = Expert, PhD

*The original kanji consisted of a smaller axe that was placed with the blade side down, giving the meaning of warrior / man.

夫 HUSBAND

"A man wearing an ornamental hairpin the day he becomes a husband (夫)"

SIMILAR KANJI	ON (フ)		Kun (おっと)
天 = Heaven 大 = Big	だいじょうぶ 大丈夫 = All right じょうぶ 丈夫 = Strong, durable	ふじん 夫人 = Wife, Mrs. ふうふ 夫婦 = Married couple	おっと 夫 = Husband

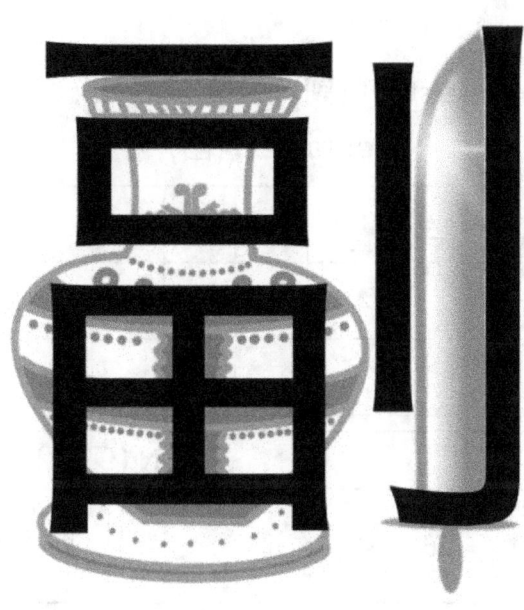
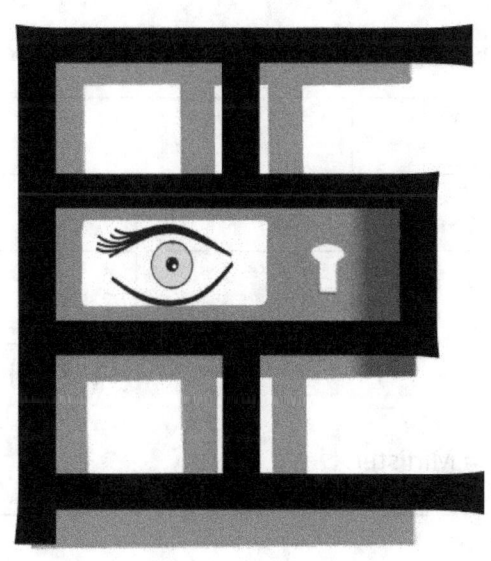

司 DIRECTOR, OFFICIAL

"I open my mouth (口) when I see the director (司) because I'm scared of him"

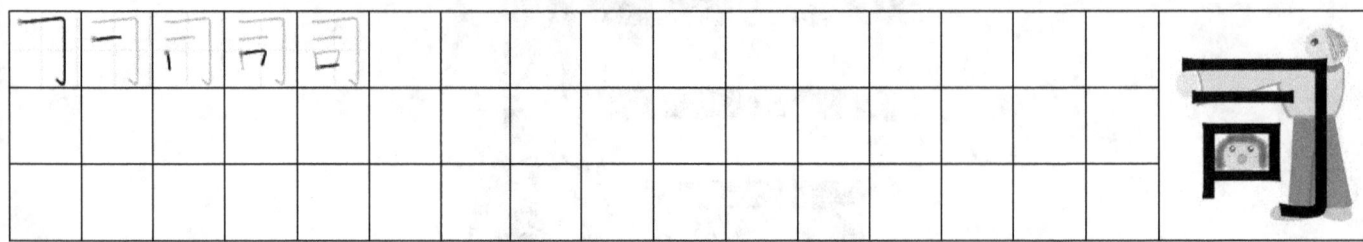

SIMILAR KANJI	ON (シ)	
同 = Same 何 = What	しかい 司会 = Chairmanship すし 寿司 = Sushi	じょうし 上司 = (One's) boss

副 ASSISTANT, AIDE

"A knife (刂) is the best assistant (副) in the kitchen; I can use it even to open containers (畐)"

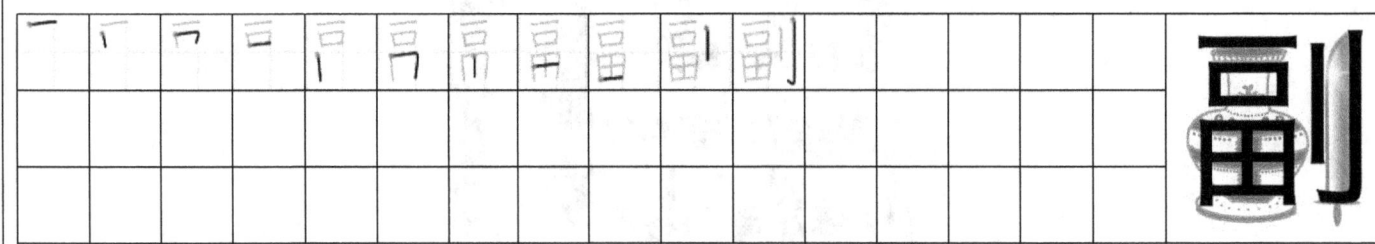

SIMILAR KANJI	ON (フク)	
富 = Wealth 福 = Blessing	ふくしょく 副食 = Side dish	ふくしょう 副賞 = Extra prize

臣 RETAINER, SUBJECT

"The retainer (臣) has his eyes wide-open and watches out for his master"

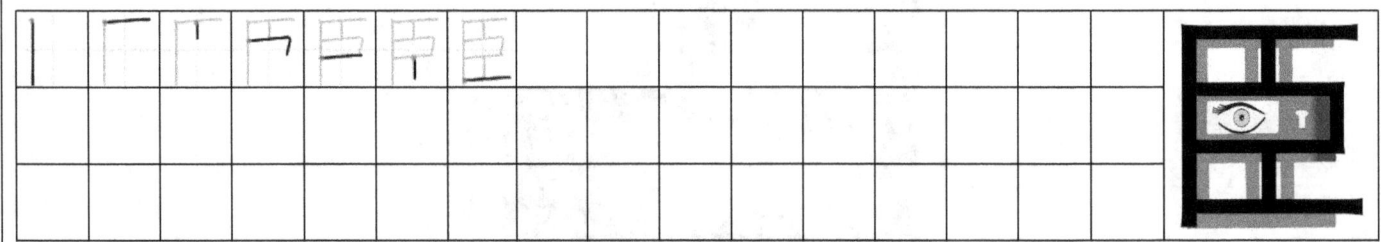

SIMILAR KANJI	ON (ジン)	
姫 = Princess 巨 = Gigantic	だいじん 大臣 = Minister	そうりだいじん 総理大臣 = Prime minister

卒 GRADUATE, SOLDIER

"This year's class will have ten (十) graduates (卒)"

SIMILAR KANJI	ON (ソツ)	
率 = Rate 傘 = Umbrella	そつぎょう 卒業 = Graduation	しんそつ 新卒 = New graduate

記 SCRIBE, NARRATIVE

"The scribe (記) is straightening (己) up his words (言) for the final speech"

SIMILAR KANJI	ON (キ)			
起 = Wake up 配 = Distribute	あんき 暗記 = Memorization きねん 記念 = Commemoration	きおく 記憶 = Memory きろく 記録 = Record	きじ 記事 = Article, news きしゃ 記者 = Reporter	にっき 日記 = Diary

博 DR., COMMAND

"The PhD (博) measures (寸) ten (十) rice fields (田) as part of his research"

SIMILAR KANJI	ON (ハク)	ODD (はか)
専 = Specialty 縛 = Arrest	はくぶつかん 博物館 = Museum	はかせ 博士 = Expert, PhD

41

客 VISITOR, GUEST

"Let the guests (客) come through the door opening (口) to stay under the roof (宀) and keep their feet (夊) warm"

SIMILAR KANJI	ON (キャク)		
各 = Each	きゃく 客 = Visitor	じょうきゃく 乗客 = Passenger	かんきゃく 観客 = Audience

君 YOU, RULER

"The ruler (君) must govern (尹) with actions, not just words from his mouth (口)"

SIMILAR KANJI	ON (クン)	Kun (きみ)
伊 = Italy 右 = Right	くん 君 = Mister	きみ 君 = You

老 OLD PERSON, GROW OLD

"The old person (老) likes sitting next to the plants (土)"

SIMILAR KANJI	ON (ロウ)	Kun (お)
考 = Consider	ろうじん 老人 = The aged, old person	お 老い = Old age, old person

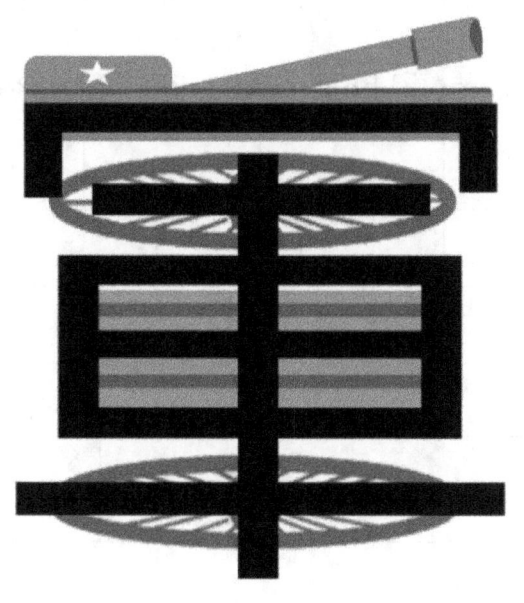

軍 ARMY
"The army (軍) cars (車) hold a good cover (冖) from the enemy"

SIMILAR KANJI	ON (グン)	
車 = Car 運 = Carry	ぐん 軍 = Army, armed forces	ぐんたい 軍隊 = Army, troops

兵 SOLDIER
"The hands (廾) of the soldier (兵) hold an axe (斤)"

SIMILAR KANJI	ON (ヘイ)	
丘 = Hill 岳 = Peak	へい 兵 = Soldier, army, troops	へいたい 兵隊 = Soldier, sailor

隊 SQUAD, CREW
"The crew (隊) sacrificed the pig (豕) for a ritual at the hill (阝)"

SIMILAR KANJI	ON (タイ)	
豚 = Pork 塚 = Hillock	ぐんたい 軍隊 = Armed forces, military	へいたい 兵隊 = Soldier, sailor

係 PERSON IN CHARGE

"In our family's lineage (系), the oldest person (亻) is the one in charge (係)"

SIMILAR KANJI	ON (ケイ)	Kun (かかり)
系 = Lineage 孫 = Grandchild	かんけい 関係 = Relationship	かかり 係 = Person in charge

治 REIGN, BE AT PEACE, HEAL, GOVERNMENT

"The government (治) from their luxurious pedestal (台), shall at least manage potable water (氵) for the nation"

SIMILAR KANJI	ON (ジ)	Kun (なお)
台 = Pedestal 始 = Begin	せいじ 政治 = Politics, government	なお 治る = To get well

官 BUREAUCRAT, THE GOVERNMENT

"The government (官) offices are under a sturdy roof (宀) for protection"

SIMILAR KANJI	ON (カン)
宮 = Shinto shrine 管 = Pipe	けいかん 警官 = Policeman

CHAPTER 4: BODY PARTS

胃	腸	脈
40	41	42
鼻	歯	身
43	44	45
指	毛	血
46	47	48

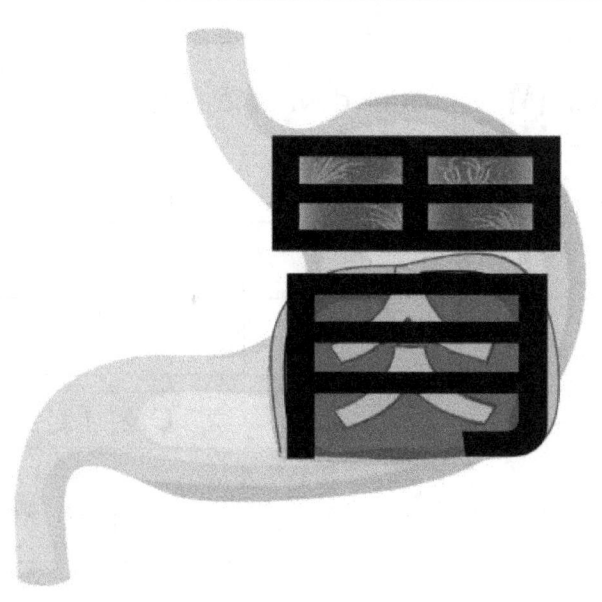

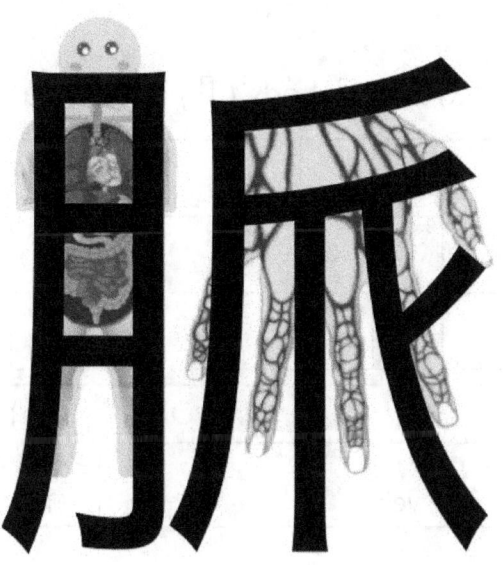

胃 STOMACH

"My stomach (胃) is irritated when eating meat (月) or rice (田)"

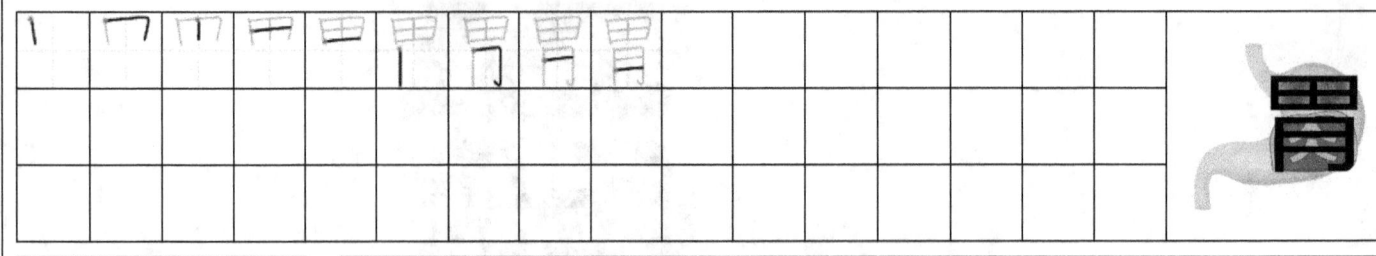

SIMILAR KANJI	ON (イ)	
冒 = Risk 畳 = Tatami mat	い 胃 = The stomach	いちょう 胃腸 = The stomach & intestines

腸 INTESTINES

"Sun (日) exposure helps protect the good bacteria of the intestines (腸)"

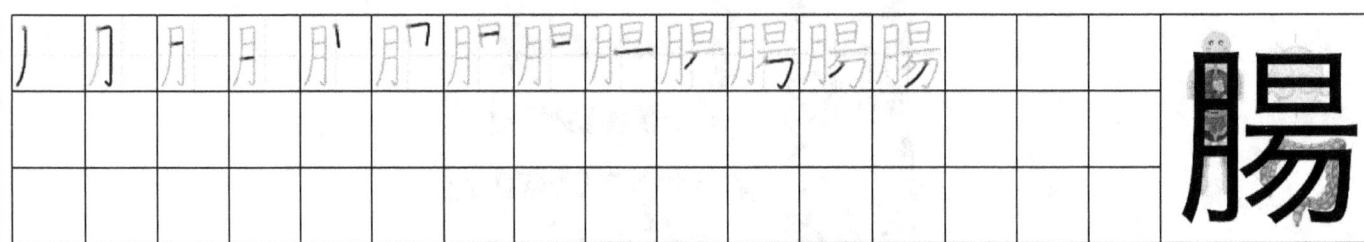

SIMILAR KANJI	ON (チョウ)	
場 = Location 揚 = Raise	ちょう 腸 = Guts, bowels, intestines	いちょう 胃腸 = The stomach & intestines

脈 VEIN

"Veins (脈) in your body (月) branch out (派)"

SIMILAR KANJI	ON (ミャク)	
派 = Faction	みゃく 脈 = Pulse, vein	みゃくはく 脈拍 = Pulse

鼻 NOSE

"I go by myself (自) to the rice field (田) and let my nose (鼻) smell the scent"

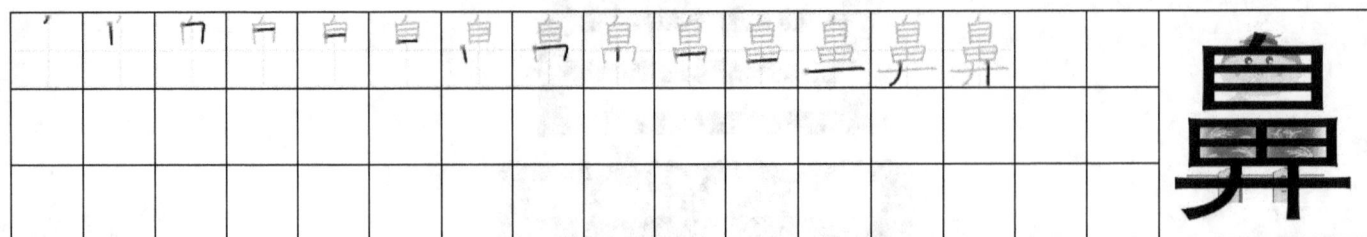

SIMILAR KANJI	Kun (はな)		
畳 = Tatami mat 胃 = Stomach	はな 鼻 = Nose	はなみず 鼻水 = Nasal mucus	はなぢ 鼻血 = Nosebleed

歯 TOOTH

"Stop (止) by the dentist often if you'd like a mouth with healthy teeth (歯)"

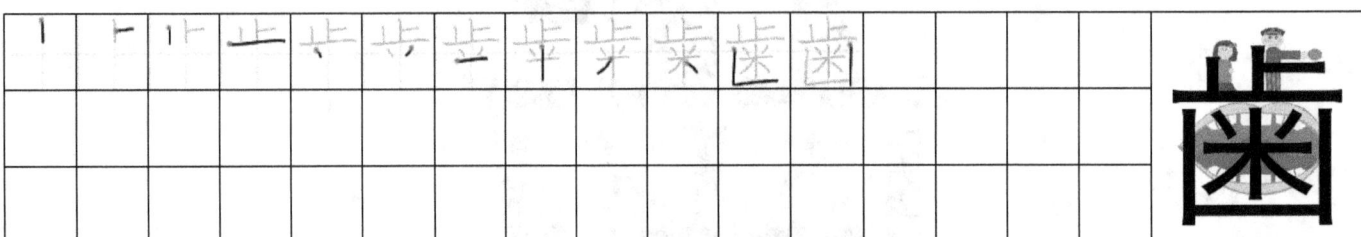

SIMILAR KANJI	ODD (は)		
奥 = Heart, interior 噛 = Chew	は 歯 = Tooth	はいしゃ 歯医者 = Dentist	むしば 虫歯 = Cavity

身 BODY, ONESELF

"The body (身) of a pregnant woman with a large belly"

SIMILAR KANJI	ON (シン)		Kun (み)
自 = Oneself 耳 = Ear	しんたい 身体 = Body しんちょう 身長 = Height	じしん 自身 = Oneself, itself しゅっしん 出身 = Person's origin	み 身 = Body, oneself

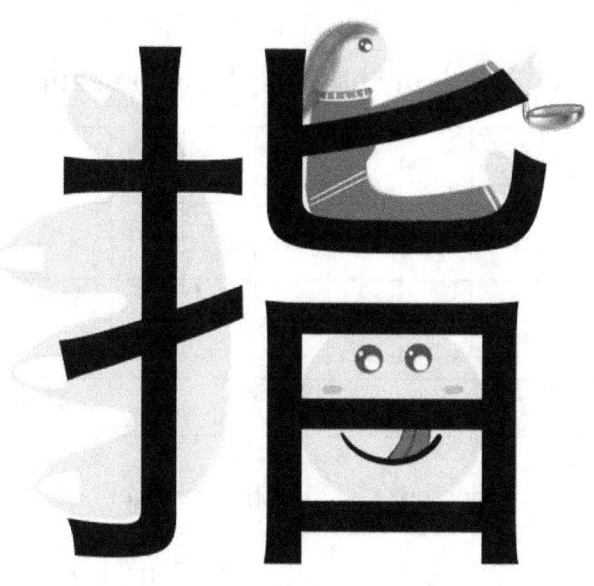

指 FINGER

"Holding a spoon (匕) with my fingers (指) while eating sweet (甘) food"

SIMILAR KANJI	ON (シ)	Kun (ゆび、さ)	
脂 = Fat, grease 旨 = Delicious	しどう 指導 = Leadership	ゆび 指 = Finger ゆびわ 指輪 = (Finger) ring	さ 指す = To point

毛 HAIR, WOOL

"A girl with very messy hair (毛)"

SIMILAR KANJI	ON (モウ)	Kun (け)	
手 = Hand 尾 = Tail	もうふ 毛布 = Blanket, rug	け 毛 = Hair, wool けがわ 毛皮 = Fur	かみ け 髪の毛 = Hair (head)

血 BLOOD

"A drop of blood (血) inside a chalice (皿) for sacrificial purposes"

SIMILAR KANJI	ON (ケツ)	Kun (ち)
皿 = Dish	けつえき 血液 = Blood	ち 血 = Blood

CHAPTER 5: NATURE

星	景	原	波	湖	汽
49	50	51	52	53	54
流	湯	陽	芽	葉	草
55	56	57	58	59	60
石	岩	島	岸	炭	畑
61	62	63	64	65	66
熱	陸	毒	農	根	松
67	68	69	70	71	72
粉	種	季	候	節	竹
73	74	75	76	77	78
雲	雪	鉄			
79	80	81			

星 STAR

"The sun (日), is a star (星) and it is essential for life (生) on earth"

SIMILAR KANJI	ON (セイ)	Kun (ほし)
呈 = Display 皇 = Emperor	えいせい 衛星 = Satellite	ほし 星 = Star

景 SCENERY, VIEW

"Beautiful scenery (景) with the capital city (京) and the sun (日) right above"

SIMILAR KANJI	ON (ケイ)	
京 = Capital 影 = Shadow	けいき 景気 = Business conditions ふうけい 風景 = Landscape, scenery	こうけい 光景 = Scene けしき 景色 = Scenery

原 FIELD

"The white (白) angel on the cliff (厂) provides a small (小) stream to irrigate the field (原)"

SIMILAR KANJI	ON (ゲン)	Kun (はら)
泉 = Fountain	げんいん 原因 = Cause, origin	はら 原 = Field

*The original meaning of this kanji was "the place where water originates", which later changed to include the surrounding area as well = field.

波 WAVE

"I love seeing beach waves (波) and the mist of the water (氵) touch my skin (皮)"

SIMILAR KANJI	ON (ハ)	Kun (なみ)
彼 = He 疲 = Tired	でんぱ 電波 = Radio wave	なみ 波 = Wave

湖 LAKE

"The water (氵) in this old (古) lake (湖) looks beautiful under the moon (月)"

SIMILAR KANJI	ON (コ)	Kun (みずうみ)
潮 = Tide 朝 = Morning	こてい 湖底 = Bottom of a lake	みずうみ 湖 = Lake

*In the original meaning, 胡 meant large, as in a "lake was a large body of water".

汽 STEAM, VAPOR

"Water (氵) forms steam (汽) in the air (气) when heated"

SIMILAR KANJI	ON (キ)
気 = Spirit	きしゃ 汽車 = Steam train

流

湯

陽

流 CURRENT, FLOW

"The child (㐬) follows the path of the water's (氵) flow (流) in the river (川)"

SIMILAR KANJI	ON (リュウ)	Kun (なが)
硫 = Sulphur 荒 = Laid waste	りゅうこう 流 行 = Fashion, trend なが 流 れる = To stream	なが 流 れ = Stream, current なが 流 す = To drain

* The element 㐬 is the kanji for child (子) but inverted.

湯 HOT WATER

"The water (氵) warmed by sun rays (昜) becomes hot water (湯)"

SIMILAR KANJI	Kun (ゆ)
場 = Location 揚 = Raise, elevate	ゆ 湯 = Hot water

陽 SUNSHINE, POSITIVE

"A beautiful image of the autumn sun rays (昜), hill (阝), and a sunshine (陽)"

SIMILAR KANJI	ON (ヨウ)
場 = Location 湯 = Hot water	ようき 陽 気 = Cheerful, weather, season　　たいよう 太 陽 = Sun, solar

芽 BUD, SPROUT

"Both, plants (艹) and teeth (牙) growth start as buds (芽)"

一 亠 艹 艹 芒 芹 芽 芽

SIMILAR KANJI	ON (ガ)	Kun (め)
芹 = Parsley 邪 = Wicked	はつが 発芽 = Germinations, sprouting	め 芽 = Sprout

葉 LEAF

"The leaves (葉) of trees (木) and plants (艹) around the world (世) are different"

一 亠 艹 艹 芹 芹 芒 苹 苹 葦 葉 葉

SIMILAR KANJI	ON (ヨウ)	Kun (は)
棄 = Abandon 菜 = Vegetable	こうよう 紅葉 = Autumn leaves はがき 葉書 = Postal card	は 葉 = Leaf ことば 言葉 = Word, language

草 GRASS, WEED

"Grass (草) needs direct sun (日) to survive and must be seeded in early (早) fall"

一 亠 艹 艹 芍 芇 苫 营 草

SIMILAR KANJI	Kun (くさ)	
早 = Early 単 = Simple	くさ 草 = Grass, weed	くさき 草木 = Plants, vegetation

石 STONE

"A stone (石) beneath a cliff (厂)"

一 丆 丆 石 石

SIMILAR KANJI	ON (セキ)		Kun (いし)
右 = Right 岩 = Rock	せきゆ 石油 = Oil, petroleum ほうせき 宝石 = Jewel, gem	せきたん 石炭 = Coal	いし 石 = Stone

岩 ROCK

"Many rocks (岩) and stones (石) build up in the mountain (山)"

丨 山 山 屵 屵 岩 岩

SIMILAR KANJI	ON (ガン)	Kun (いわ)
石 = Stone 岸 = Beach	ようがん 溶岩 = Lava	いわ 岩 = Rock

島 ISLAND

"This is a view of mountains (山) and birds (鳥) perching on a famous island (島)"

丿 亻 冂 卢 自 鸟 鸟 島 島 島

SIMILAR KANJI	ON (トウ)	Kun (しま)
鳥 = Bird 馬 = Horse	むじんとう 無人島 = Desert island	しま 島 = Island, isle

岸 BEACH

"A mountain (山) cliff (厂) view with a beach (岸) and dry (干) air"

SIMILAR KANJI	ON (ガン)	Kun (きし)
炭 = Charcoal 岩 = Rock	かいがん 海岸 = Coast	きし 岸 = Bank, shore

炭 CHARCOAL

"The fire (火) at the mountain (山) cliff (厂) left charcoal (炭) residue"

SIMILAR KANJI	ON (タン)	Kun (すみ)
岸 = Beach 灰 = Ashes	せきたん 石炭 = Coal	すみ 炭 = Charcoal

畑 FIELD, FARM

"Removing crop residues in the rice field (田) farm (畑) with fire (火)"

SIMILAR KANJI	Kun (はたけ)
細 = Narrow	はたけ 畑 = Field

熱 HEAT, TEMPERATURE

"The curled up (丸) person adds plants (土) to the fire (灬) to raise the temperature (熱)"

SIMILAR KANJI	ON (ネツ)		Kun (あつ)
勢 = Forces, energy 熟 = Mellow, ripen	ねっしん 熱心 = Zeal, enthusiasm ねったい 熱帯 = Tropics	ねっちゅう 熱中 = Mania ねつ 熱 = Fever	あつ 熱い = Hot (thing)

陸 LAND

"A land (陸) with hills (阝) and grass (土) spread throughout"

SIMILAR KANJI	ON (リク)	
陵 = Mausoleum 階 = Stair	りく 陸 = Land, shore	たいりく 大陸 = Continent

毒 POISON

"The mother (母) protects her child from the poisonous (毒) plants (龶)"

SIMILAR KANJI	ON (ドク)	
毎 = Every 母 = Mother	きどく 気の毒 = Pitiful, unfortunate	どく 毒 = Poison

農 AGRICULTURE, FARMERS

"Doing agriculture (農) work at the rice paddies (田) with a garden fork (辰)"

SIMILAR KANJI	ON (ノウ)		
濃 = Thick	のうぎょう 農業 = Agriculture	のうみん 農民 = Farmers	のうか 農家 = Farmhouse

*This kanji originally had multiple rice paddies and trees. It now looks like the unrelated kanji of 曲 (bend / tune).

根 ROOT

"A good (艮) root (根) will make a strong tree (木)"

SIMILAR KANJI	Kun (ね)	
恨 = Regret 眼 = Eyeball	ね 根 = Root	やね 屋根 = Roof

松 PINE TREE

"Pine trees (松) are trees (木) often used in public (公) gardens and parks"

SIMILAR KANJI	Kun (まつ)
公 = Public 校 = School	まつ 松 = Pine tree

粉

種

季

粉 POWDER

"Let's divide (分) the rice (米) grains and make it into fine powder (粉)"

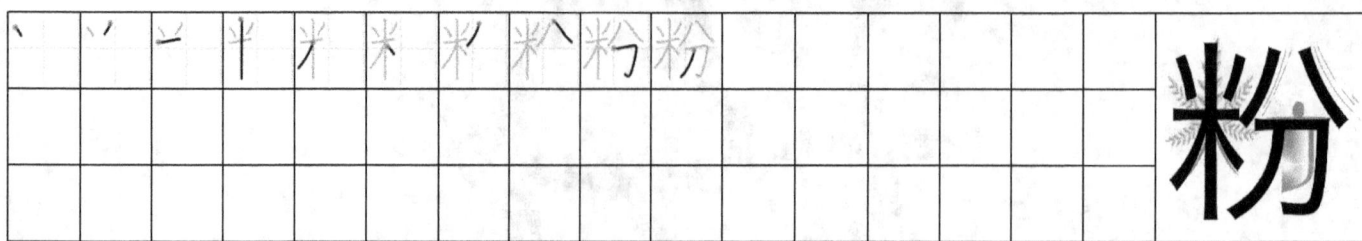

SIMILAR KANJI	ON (フン)	Kun (こな)
紛 = Distract 粒 = Grains	かふん 花粉 = Pollen	こな 粉 = Powder, dust

種 SEED

"Heavy (重) grains (禾) and seeds (種) are the best to harvest"

SIMILAR KANJI	ON (シュ)		Kun (たね)
重 = Heavy	しゅるい 種類 = Variety, kind じんしゅ 人種 = Race (of people)	いっしゅ 一種 = Species, kind	たね 種 = Seed, cause

季 SEASON

"Both children (子) and grains (禾) grow as the seasons (季) pass by"

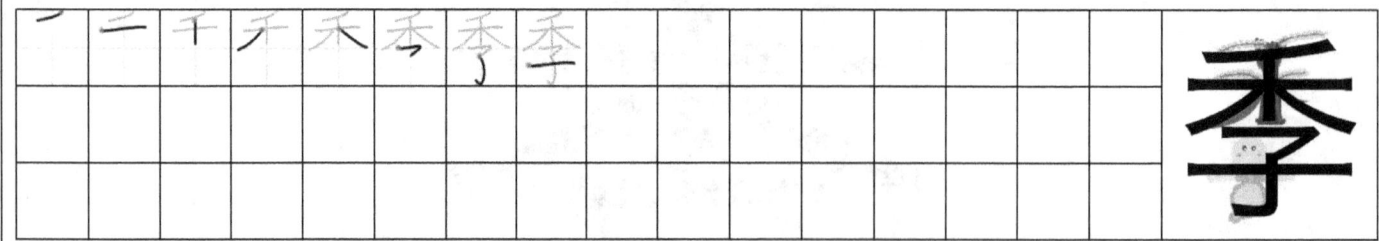

SIMILAR KANJI	ON (キ)	
委 = Committee 柔 = Tender	きせつ 季節 = Season	しき 四季 = The four seasons

候

節

竹

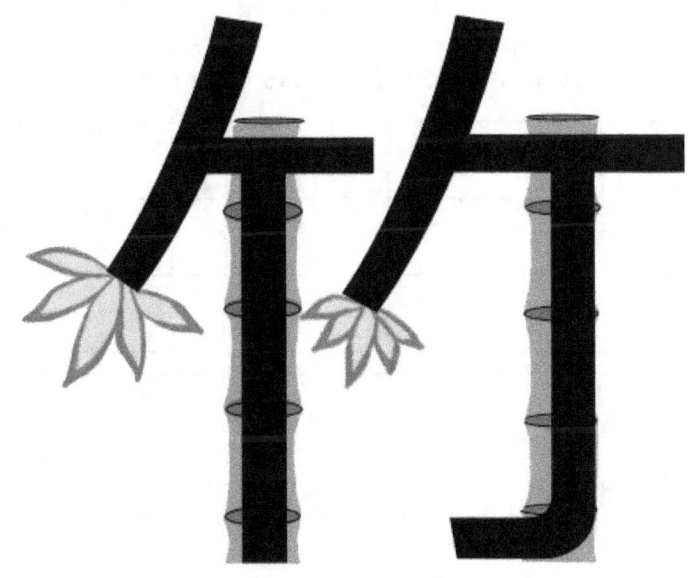

候 CLIMATE, SEASON

"A person (亻) verifies it is the season (候) to shoot arrows (矢) at the cliff (厂)"

SIMILAR KANJI	ON (コウ)		
侯 = Marquis	こうほ 候補 = Candidate	きこう 気候 = Climate	てんこう 天候 = Weather

*The original meaning of this kanji was arrow target.

節 SEASON, TUNE

"Let's celebrate the new season (節) with bamboo (⺮) instruments and kneeling down (卩) while being thankful for our food (艮)"

SIMILAR KANJI	ON (セツ)		Kun (ふし)
箱 = Box 筋 = Muscle	せつやく 節約 = Economy, saving	きせつ 季節 = Season	ふし 節 = Melody, tune

竹 BAMBOO

"Two bamboo (竹) stalks with leaves"

SIMILAR KANJI	Kun (たけ)
干 = Dry	たけ 竹 = Bamboo

雲

雪

鉄

雲 CLOUD

"Too many dark clouds (云) together means that it is going to rain (雨)"

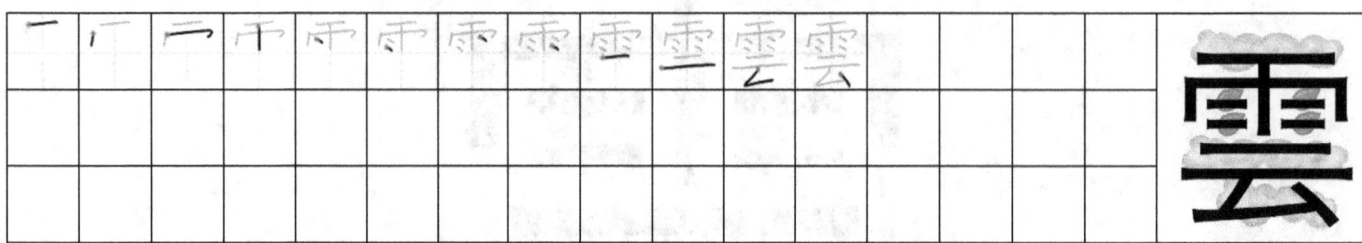

SIMILAR KANJI	Kun (くも)
雷 = Thunder 震 = Shake, tremble	くも 雲 = Cloud

雪 SNOW

"I love sticking out my hand (ヨ) when it rains (雨) or snows (雪)"

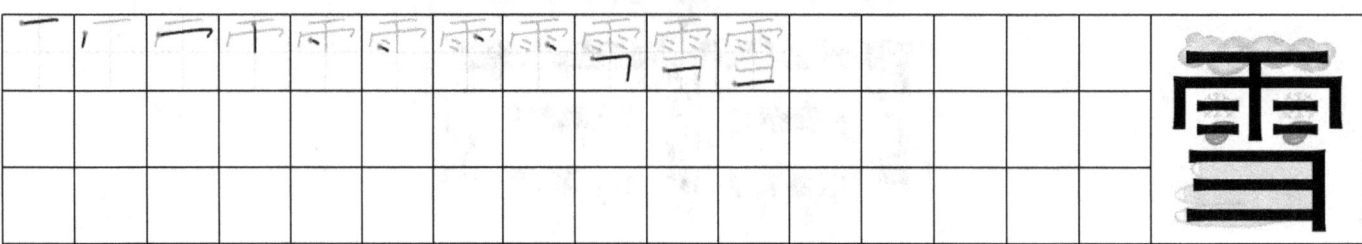

SIMILAR KANJI	Kun (ゆき)
雷 = Thunder 雨 = Rain	ゆき 雪 = Snow

* The original kanji had a hand with a broom to give a meaning of the snow cleaning the ground.

鉄 IRON

"I've lost (失) my metal (金) collar made out of iron (鉄)"

SIMILAR KANJI	ON (テツ)	
失 = Lose, error 秩 = Regularity	てつ 鉄 = Iron ちかてつ 地下鉄 = Underground railway	てつどう 鉄道 = Rail line

CHAPTER 6: OBJECTS

玉	球	柱	機	械	材
82	83	84	85	86	87
札	標	票	帯	席	帳
88	89	90	91	92	93
糸	絵	束	船	器	荷
94	95	96	97	98	99
賞	貸	管	筆	箱	笛
100	101	102	103	104	105
矢	弓	刀	具	旗	輪
106	107	108	109	110	111
型	坂	印	灯	皿	衣
112	113	114	115	116	117
鏡	面	角			
118	119	120			

玉 JEWEL, BALL
"The king (王) protects the country's jewels (玉)"

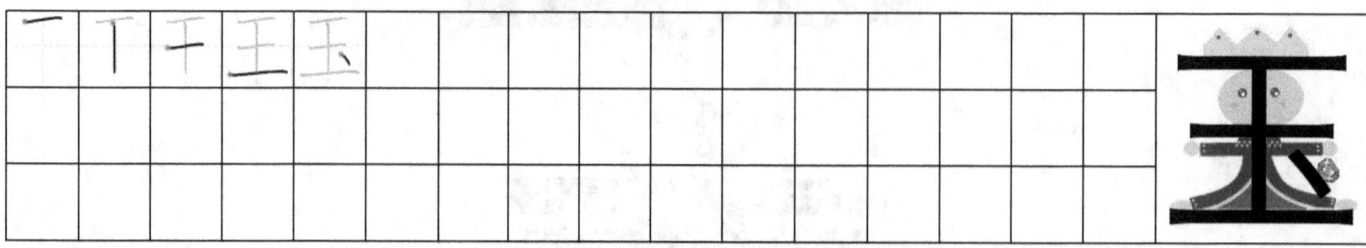

SIMILAR KANJI	Kun (たま)	
王 = King 宝 = Treasure	たま 玉 = Ball	たまねぎ 玉ネギ = Onion

球 SPHERE
"The peasant is requesting (求) the golden sphere (球) from the king (王)"

SIMILAR KANJI	ON (キュウ)	Kun (たま)
求 = Request	きゅう 球 = Globe, sphere ちきゅう 地球 = Earth	たま 球 = Globe, sphere

柱 PILLAR, COLUMN
"Both a tree (木) and a master chief (主) can act as a pillar (柱) for the nation"

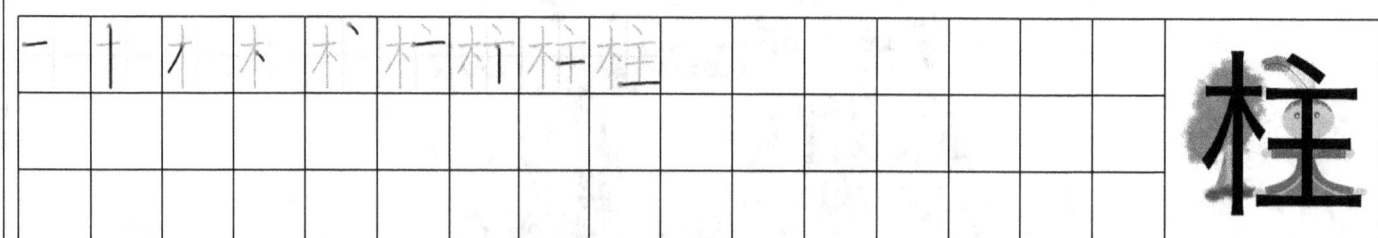

SIMILAR KANJI	Kun (はしら)
注 = Pour, irrigate 住 = Dwell, reside	はしら 柱 = Pillar

機
械
材

機 MACHINE, DEVICE, LOOM

"A person (人) cuts wood (木) with a halberd (戈) to build a yarn (丝) machine (機)"

SIMILAR KANJI	ON (キ)		
幾 = How many 磯 = Seashore	きかい 機械 = Machine ひこうき 飛行機 = Airplane	きかん 機関 = Mechanism, engine きのう 機能 = Function, faculty	きげん 機嫌 = Temper, mood

械 MACHINE, GADGET

"The first machines (械) were made out of wood (木) and were built to punish (戒) people"

SIMILAR KANJI	ON (カイ)	
戒 = Commandment, punish	きかい 機械 = Machine	きかい 器械 = Instrument

材 LUMBER, LOG, TIMBER, MATERIAL

"You don't have to be a genius (才) to realize how many raw materials (材) you can get from trees (木)"

SIMILAR KANJI	ON (ザイ)
村 = Village 才 = Genius	ざいりょう 材料 = Ingredients

札 TOKEN, BANKNOTE

"Please straighten the bent (乚) pieces of wood (木) and make tokens (札)"

SIMILAR KANJI	ON (サツ)
礼 = Salute 机 = Desk	さつ 札　= Token, ticket

標 SIGNPOST, LABEL

"That tree (木) is a signpost (標) where lucky tickets (票) get dropped off"

SIMILAR KANJI	ON (ヒョウ)
漂 = Drift 徳 = Benevolence	もくひょう 目　標　= Mark, target

票 BALLOT, TICKET

"Place your lucky tickets (票) on the altar (示)"

SIMILAR KANJI	ON (ヒョウ)
標 = Sign 漂 = Drift	とうひょう 投　票　= Voting, poll

* For this kanji specifically, 示 had more the form of fire than that of an altar.

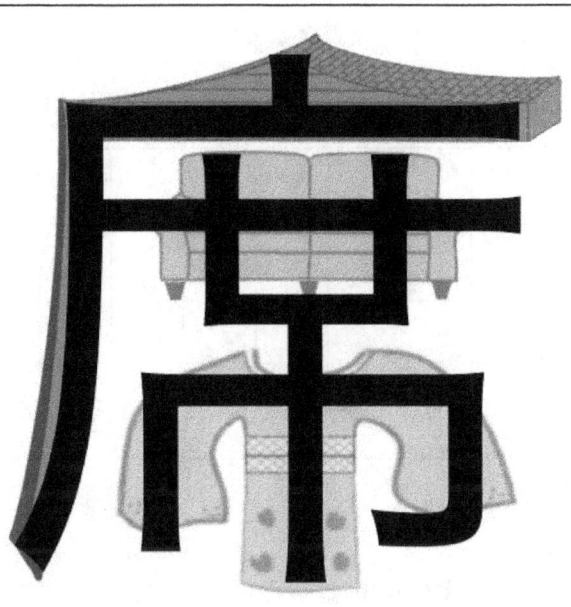

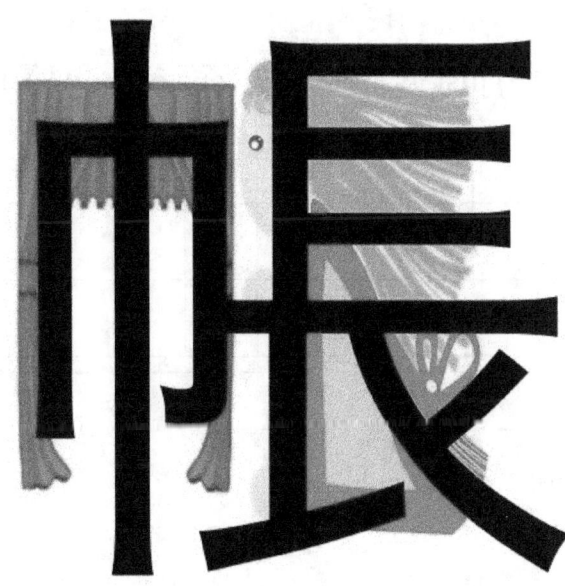

帯 SASH, ZONE

"An accessory that helps keep clothes (巾) on is a sash (帯)"

SIMILAR KANJI	ON (タイ)	Kun (おび)
革 = Leather 帝 = Sovereign	ねったい 熱帯 = Tropics	おび 帯 = Sash, obi

席 SEAT

"In the seamstress tent (广), there is a rare cloth (巾) laying on her seat (席)"

SIMILAR KANJI	ON (セキ)	
度 = Degrees 渡 = Transit	けっせき 欠席 = Absence しゅっせき 出席 = Attendance	ざせき 座席 = Seat

帳 CURTAIN, NOTEBOOK

"This curtain (帳) just looks like a piece of long (長) cloth (巾)"

SIMILAR KANJI	ON (チョウ)	
張 = Lengthen 脹 = Dilate	つうちょう 通帳 = Passbook	てちょう 手帳 = Notebook

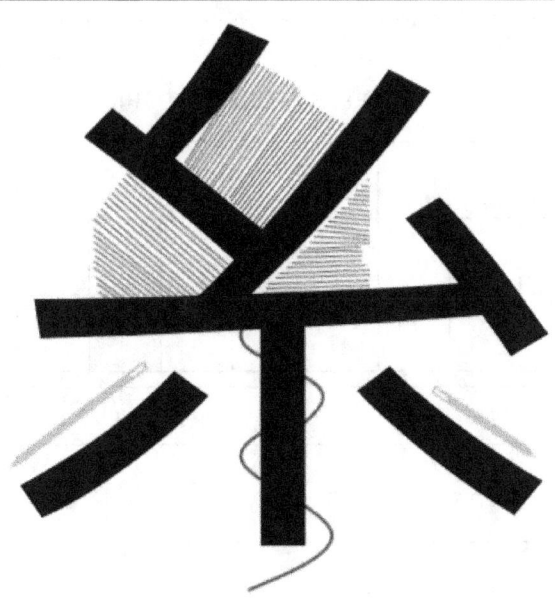

糸 YARN, THREAD

"Yarn (糸) made of silk"

SIMILAR KANJI	Kun (いと)	
系 = Lineage 孫 = Grandchild	いと 糸 = Yarn	けいと 毛糸 = Knitting wool

絵 PAINTING

"Meet (会) the person that can create paintings (絵) by using colorful yarns (糸)"

SIMILAR KANJI	ON (エ、カイ)	
会 = Meeting 給 = Salary	え 絵 = Picture, drawing	かいが 絵画 = Picture

*The origin of this kanji was about pulling threads of different colors, which eventually came to mean "painting".

束 BUNDLE, BUNCH

"Get a big bundle (束) of firewood from broken trees (木)"

SIMILAR KANJI	ON (ソク)	Kun (たば)
東 = East	やくそく 約束 = Promise, engagement	たば 束 = Bundle, bunch

船 SHIP

"A ship (船) travels more efficiently along (㕣) with the water than a boat (舟)"

SIMILAR KANJI	ON (セン)	Kun (ふね)
沿 = Run alongside 鉛 = Lead	ふうせん 風船 = Balloon, airship	ふね 船 = Ship

器 VESSEL

"A big (大) person is guarding four vessels (器)"

SIMILAR KANJI	ON (キ)	
品 = Goods	きよう 器用 = Skillful, handy	ぶき 武器 = Weapon

*The original kanji had the element of a dog (犬) instead of big (大)

荷 BAGAGGE, LOAD

"What (何) is in your baggage (荷)? I always pack my plants (艹) first"

SIMILAR KANJI	Kun (に)
何 = What 伺 = Pay respects	にもつ 荷物 = Luggage

*The plant 艹 radical in this kanji came from a comparison with lotus plants, as they are upright and look like they are carrying a load.

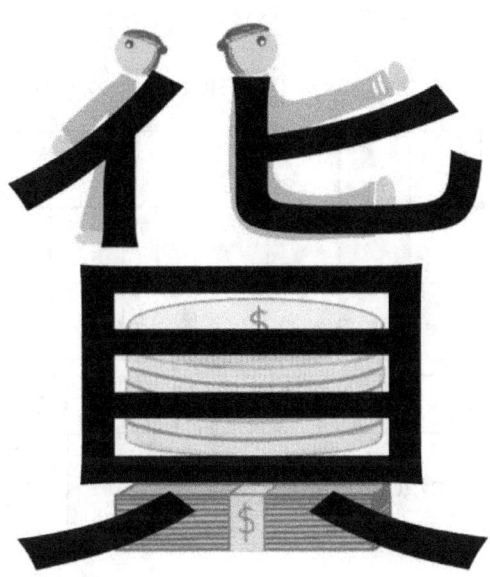

賞 PRIZE

"The prize (賞) for his hard work was making good money (貝) and getting a high status (尚) home"

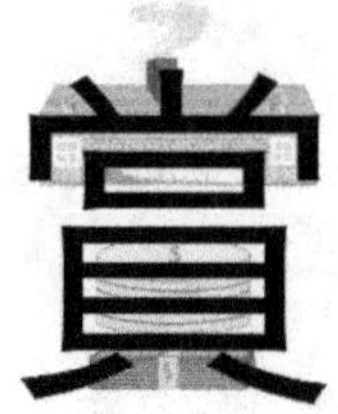

SIMILAR KANJI
員 = Employee
償 = Reparation

ON (ショウ)
しょう
賞 = Prize, award

しょうきん
賞金 = Prize money

貨 GOODS, FREIGHT

"Every day we change (化) money (貝) into goods (貨)"

SIMILAR KANJI
貸 = Lend
賃 = Fare

ON (カ)
かもつ
貨物 = Cargo, freight

こうか
硬貨 = Coin

管 PIPE

"The pipes (管) at the government office (官) are made out of bamboo (⺮) stalk"

SIMILAR KANJI
官 = Bureaucrat
筒 = Cylinder

ON (カン)
かんり
管理 = Control, management

Kun (くだ)
くだ
管 = Pipe, tube

筆 WRITING BRUSH

"The best writing brush (筆) is a brush (聿) made out of bamboo (⺮)"

SIMILAR KANJI	ON (ヒツ)	Kun (ふで)
書 = Writing	えんぴつ 鉛筆 = Pencil まんねんひつ 万年筆 = Fountain pen	ふで 筆 = Writing brush

箱 BOX, CHEST

"Boxes (箱) made of Bamboo (⺮) used to be hung facing each other (相) on either side of a horse carriage"

SIMILAR KANJI	Kun (はこ)
相 = Mutual 想 = Think	はこ 箱 = Box

笛 FLUTE

"Some flutes (笛) are made out of bamboo (⺮) and look like an empty gourd (由) with holes"

SIMILAR KANJI	Kun (ふえ)
宙 = Space 由 = A reason	ふえ 笛 = Flute

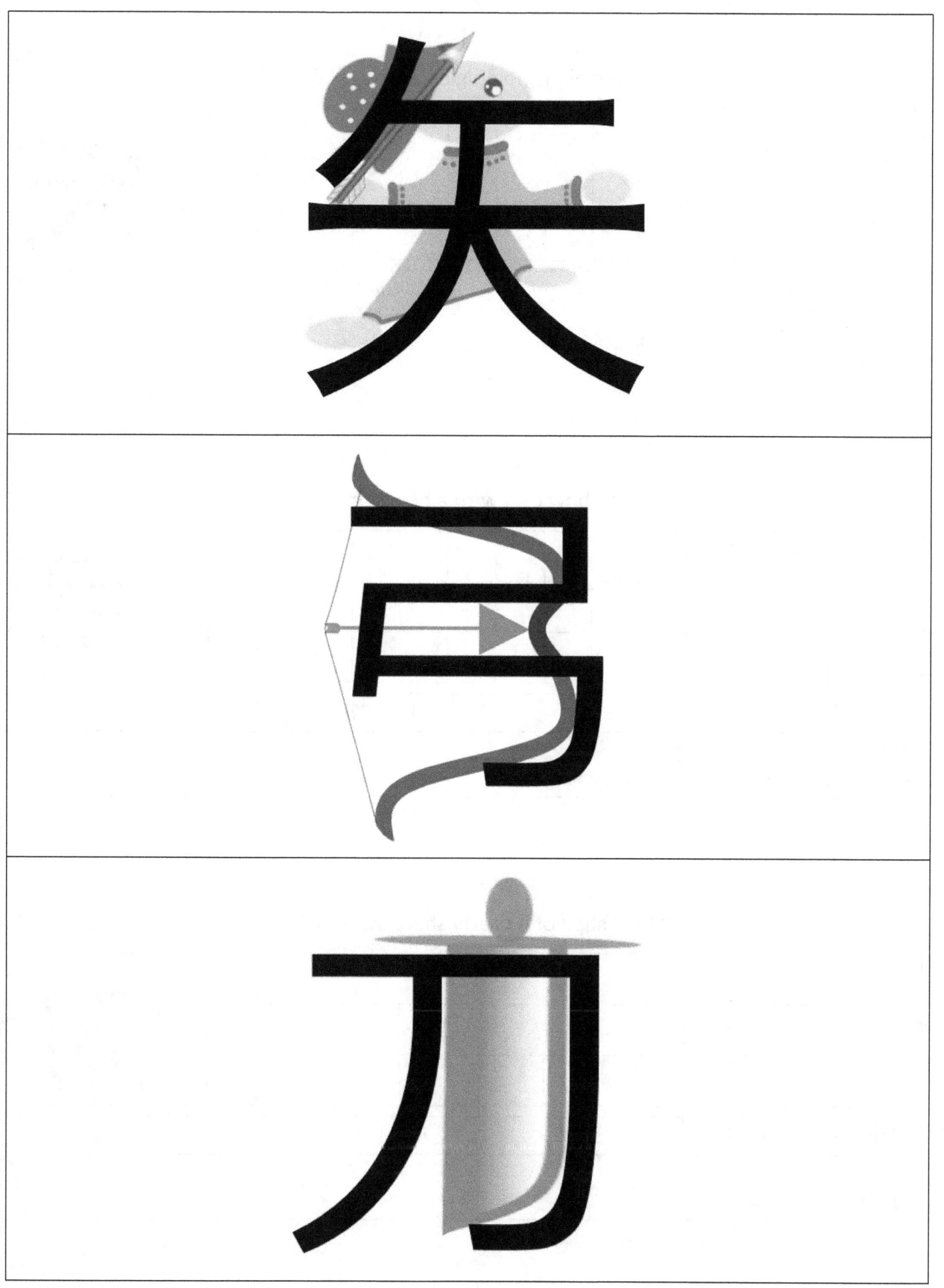

矢 ARROW

"The girl is holding an arrow (矢)"

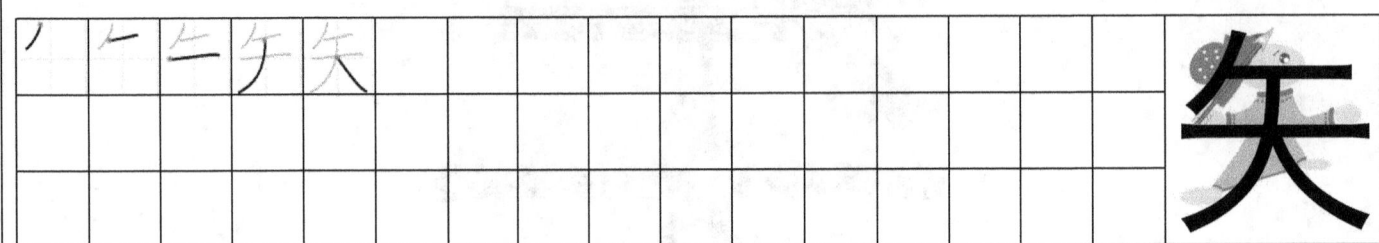

SIMILAR KANJI	Kun (や)
医 = Medicine, doctor 知 = Know	やじるし 矢 印 = Arrow (symbol)

弓 BOW

"A bow (弓) with a bowstring"

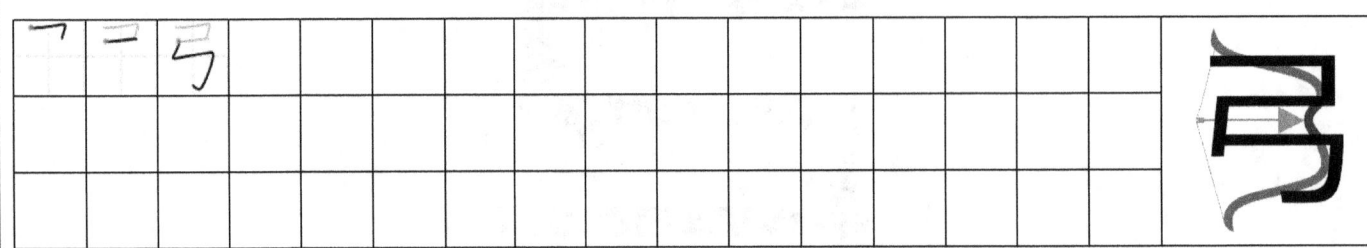

SIMILAR KANJI	Kun (ゆみ)
引 = Pull 弔 = Condolences	ゆみ 弓 = Bow

刀 SWORD

"The shape of a pretty sharp sword (刀)"

SIMILAR KANJI	Kun (かたな)
九 = Nine 刃 = Blade	かたな 刀 = Sword

具 TOOL, UTENSIL

"A vessel was used as a tool (具) for offerings"

SIMILAR KANJI	ON (グ)	
見 = See 貝 = Shellfish	かぐ 家具 = Furniture ぐあい 具合 = Condition, health	ぐたい 具体 = Concrete, tangible

旗 FLAG

"The person is setting up a flag (旗) pole (㫃) right above the basket (其)"

SIMILAR KANJI	Kun (はた)
旅 = Trip 旋 = Rotation	はた 旗 = Flag

輪 WHEEL

"Getting the cart (車) and wheels (輪) ready to carry big volumes of books (冊)"

SIMILAR KANJI	Kun (わ)	
倫 = Ethics 論 = Argument	わ 輪 = Ring, hoop	ゆびわ 指輪 = (Finger) ring

剗

板

卬

型 MOLD

"We are making a mold (型) with soil (土), a knife (刀), and two poles (开)"

一	二	于	开	刑	刑	型	型	型				

SIMILAR KANJI	ON (ケイ)	Kun (かた)
刑 = Punish 形 = Shape	てんけい 典型 = Type, pattern	かた 型 = Mold, model

板 BOARD, PLANK

"Trees (木) are widely used for making planks (板) strong enough to lean against (反)"

一	十	才	木	朽	朽	板	板					

SIMILAR KANJI	ON (バン)	Kun (いた)
坂 = Slope 返 = Return	こくばん 黒板 = Blackboard	いた 板 = Board, plank

印 SEAL

"A hand (⺕) pushing down a kneeling person (卩) was a sign of pressing a seal (印) down"

′	⺁	F	E	臼	印							

SIMILAR KANJI	ON (イン)		Kun (しるし)
卵 = Egg 即 = Instant	いんさつ 印刷 = Printing	いんしょう 印象 = Impression	しるし 印 = Mark

灯 LAMP

"Fire (火) lamps (灯) were used to light up the streets (丁)"

SIMILAR KANJI	ON (トウ)		Kun (ひ)
丁 = Street 町 = Town	とうだい 灯台 = Lighthouse	でんとう 電灯 = Electric light	ひ 灯 = Lamp

* The original Kanji was 燈 which was fire next to a lamp with a tray.

皿 DISH, PLATE

"A concave dish (皿)"

SIMILAR KANJI	Kun (さら)	
血 = Blood 且 = Moreover	さら 皿 = Plate, dish	はいざら 灰皿 = Ashtray

衣 CLOTHES

"Showing off in these pretty clothes (衣)"

SIMILAR KANJI	ON (イ)	ODD (た)
依 = Reliant 表 = Surface	いふく 衣服 = Clothes	ゆかた 浴衣 = Yukata

鏡

面

角

鏡 MIRROR

"I'm standing (立) here looking (見) at myself in the mirror (鏡) with the metal (金) frame"

SIMILAR KANJI	ODD (カネ)	Kun (かがみ)
境 = Boundary	めがね 眼鏡 = Glasses	かがみ 鏡 = Mirror

面 MASK, FACE

"A man in a mask (面), with a big eye (目)"

SIMILAR KANJI	ON (メン)		ODD (じ)
画 = Picture	めん 面 = Face ばめん 場面 = Scene	めんどう 面倒 = Trouble ひょうめん 表面 = Surface	まじめ 真面目 = Diligent, serious

角 ANGLE, CORNER, HORN

"Looking at the weird angle (角) of a very old horn (角)"

SIMILAR KANJI	Kun (かど、すの)	
負 = Defeat 用 = Utilize	かど 角 = Corner	つの 角 = Horn

CHAPTER 7: PLACES

庫	庭	府	園	坂	街
121	122	123	124	125	126
戸	局	橋	倉	宮	宿
127	128	129	130	131	132
公	谷	路	郡	部	階
133	134	135	136	137	138
港	州	科	丁	寺	里
139	140	141	142	143	144

庫 WAREHOUSE, DEPOSITORY

"A warehouse (庫) under a tent (广) can be used as a garage for cars (車)"

SIMILAR KANJI	ON (コ)	
車 = Car	きんこ 金庫 = Safe, vault	れいぞうこ 冷蔵庫 = Refrigerator

庭 COURTYARD, GARDEN

"The garden (庭) under the tent (广) belongs to the royal court (廷)"

SIMILAR KANJI	ON (テイ)	Kun (にわ)
延 = Prolong 廷 = Court	かてい 家庭 = Home, family	にわ 庭 = Garden

*Originally the garden was a place where the god of earth was worshipped.

府 GOVERNMENT OFFICE, PREFECTURE

"The government office (府) ensures people adhere (付) to rules"

SIMILAR KANJI	ON (フ)
付 = Adhere 符 = Token	せいふ 政府 = Government

園 GARDEN, PLANTATION

"The school garden (園) is in a big enclosure (口). There, kids get their clothes (衣) dirty with soil (土)"

SIMILAR KANJI	ON (エン)	
遠 = Far 猿 = Monkey	こうえん 公園 = (Public) park	どうぶつえん 動物園 = Zoo

坂 SLOPE

"The hand (又) is trying to reach the slope (坂) made of the soil (土)"

SIMILAR KANJI	Kun (さか)
仮 = Interim 板 = Plank	さか 坂 = Slope

街 TOWN

"The town (街) has enough soil (土) to build homes and roads (彳)"

SIMILAR KANJI	Kun (まち)	
術 = Art 掛 = Hang	まち 街 = Town	まちかど 街角 = Street corner

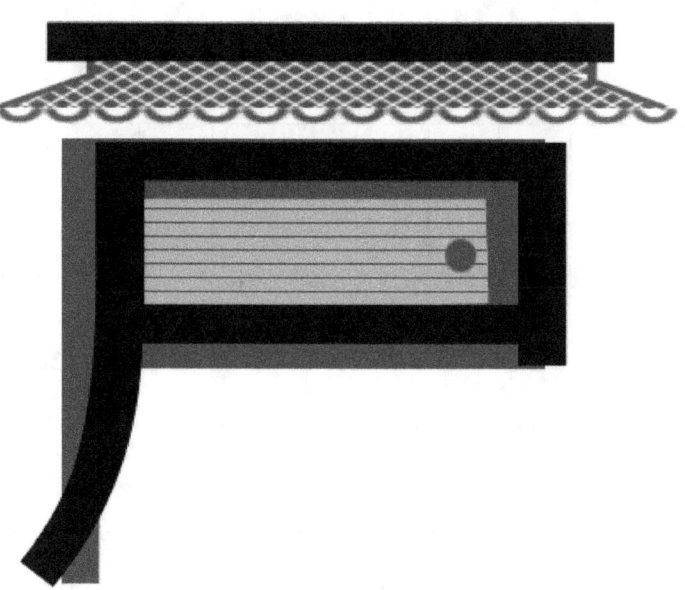

戸 DOOR
"A single door (戸) that swings"

SIMILAR KANJI	Kun (と)
声 = Voice 所 = Place	と 戸 = Door (Japanese style)

局 BUREAU, OFFICE
"The main entrance for the bureau (局) has an opening (口) with an awning (尸)"

SIMILAR KANJI	ON (キョク)		
民 = Citizen 居 = Reside	きょく 局 = Bureau	ゆうびんきょく 郵便局 = Post office	けっきょく 結局 = In the end

*The original meaning of this kanji was chessboard.

橋 BRIDGE
"This bridge (橋) is a high (喬) structure made out of wood (木)"

SIMILAR KANJI	Kun (はし)
矯 = Rectify 喬 = High	はし 橋 = Bridge

倉 STOREHOUSE

"The storehouse (倉) helps protect the harvest, and through the small opening (口) we can get what we need"

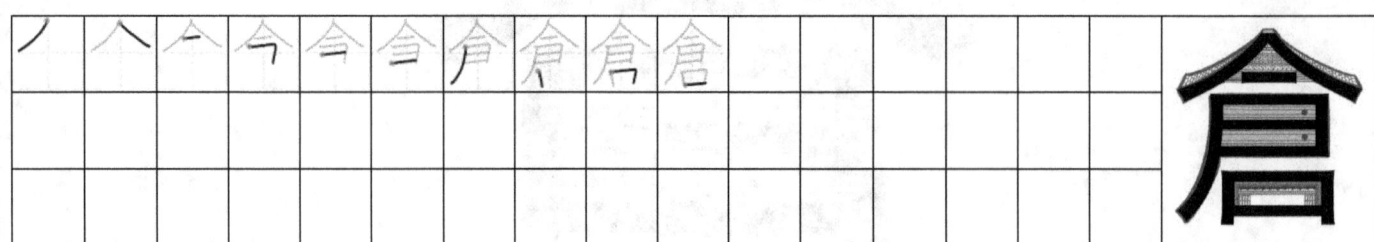

SIMILAR KANJI	Kun (ソウ)
含 = Contain 合 = Fit	そうこ 倉庫 = Storehouse, warehouse

宮 SHRINE, PALACE

"The palace (宮) has many rooms (呂) under a single roof (宀)"

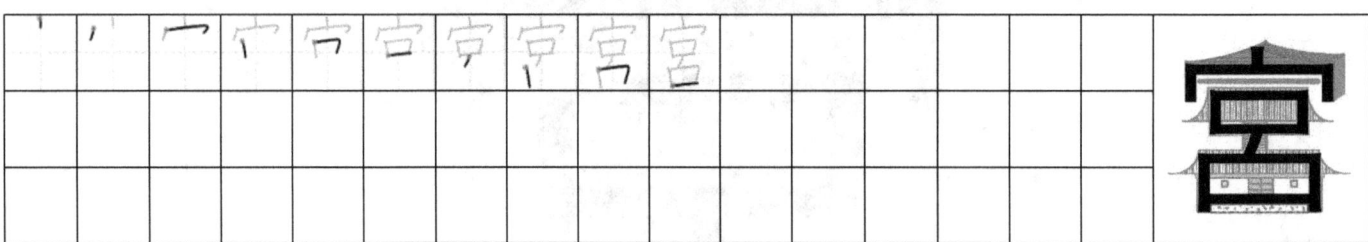

SIMILAR KANJI	ON (キュウ)
呂 = Spine 官 = Bureaucrat	おうきゅう 王宮 = Royal Palace

宿 LODGING, INN

"The person (亻) must pay 100 (百) yen to stay in the inn (宿)"

SIMILAR KANJI	ON (シュク)		Kun (やど)
縮 = Shrink	しゅくはく 宿泊 = Lodging げしゅく 下宿 = Boarding	しゅくだい 宿題 = Homework	やど 宿 = Inn, lodging

*The original kanji had "meat" instead of "one hundred" to give the meaning of "traveler".

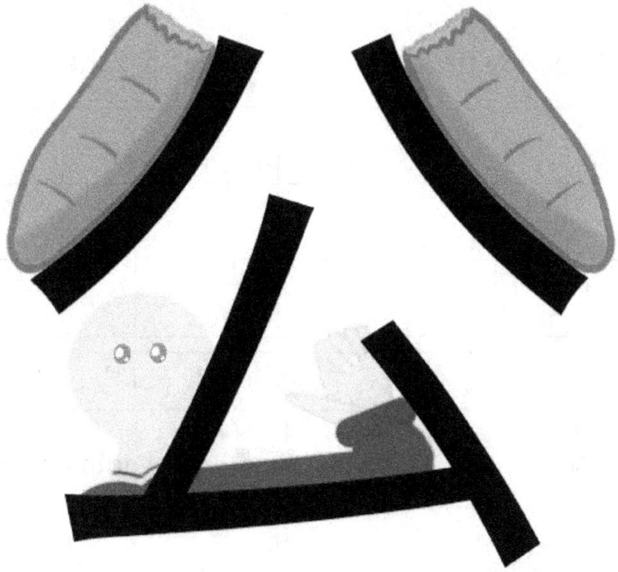

公

谷

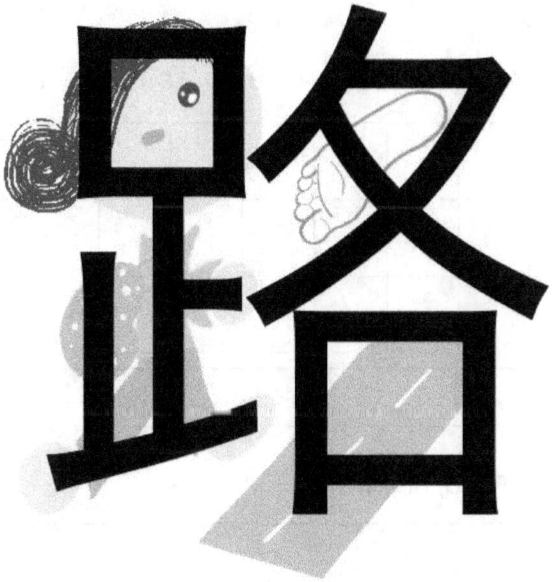

路

公 PUBLIC

"I (ム) will equally divide (八) resources for the public (公)"

SIMILAR KANJI	ON (コウ)		
松 = Pine 分 = Divide	こうえん 公園 = (Public) park	こうむいん 公務員 = Government worker	こうへい 公平 = Impartial

*The original kanji seemed to have had "table" instead of "I". This origin gives more sense to dividing resources.

谷 VALLEY

"A valley (谷) with mountain ridges (八) and the mouth (口) of a river"

SIMILAR KANJI	Kun (たに)
合 = Fit 浴 = Bathe	たに 谷 = Valley

路 PATH, ROUTE

"My legs (足) and my feet (夂) are ready to follow the next path (路)"

SIMILAR KANJI	ON (ロ)
格 = Status 略 = Abbreviation	どうろ 道路 = Road, highway

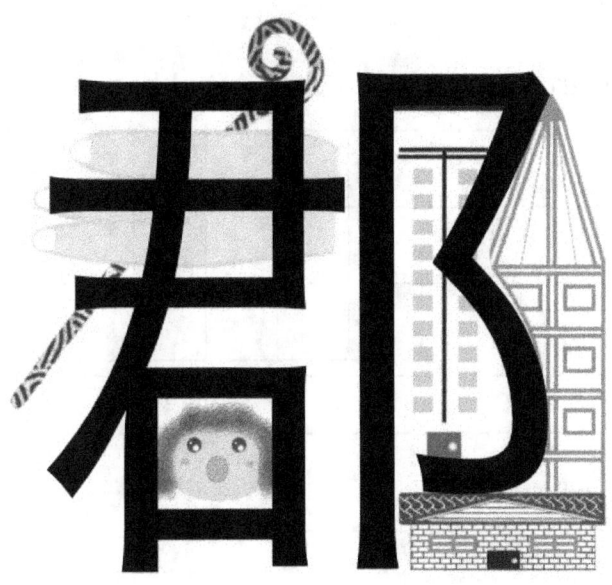

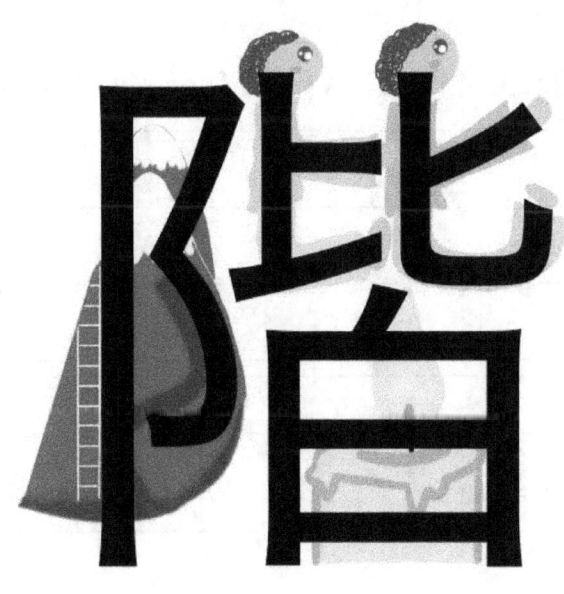

郡 DISTRICT

"The ruler (君) governs not only the village (阝) but the whole district (郡)"

SIMILAR KANJI	ON (グン)
部 = Section, bureau 都 = Capital	ぐん 郡 = District

部 SECTION, BUREAU

"The village (阝) splits (咅) into sections (部) just like plants do"

SIMILAR KANJI	ON (ブ)		ODD (ヘ)
郡 = District 都 = Capital	だいぶぶん 大部分 = Majority ぶちょう 部長 = Head of a section	ぜんぶ 全部 = All	へや 部屋 = Room

* The element 咅 is originally a seed that was about to split.

階 STAIRS

"Everyone (皆) is guided up the stairs (階) of the hill (阝) by a white (白) light"

SIMILAR KANJI	ON (カイ)	
皆 = Everyone 陸 = Land	かいだん 階段 = Stairs	にかいだ 二階建て = Two storied building

港 HARBOR, PORT

"Many people come together (共) to see the water (氵) at the port (港)"

SIMILAR KANJI	ON (コウ)	Kun (みなと)
湾 = Gulf 巻 = Scroll	くうこう 空港 = Airport	みなと 港 = Harbor

州 SANDBANK, STATE

"A sandbank (州) is a deposit of sand in a shallow area in a river (川)"

SIMILAR KANJI	ON (シユウ)
川 = River 洲 = Continent	しゅう 州 = Sandbank

科 DEPARTMENT, COURSE, SECTION

"A measuring ladle (斗) is used to sort out various types of grains (禾), which then get sent to different sections (科) for further processing"

SIMILAR KANJI	ON (カ)		
料 = Fee, materials 利 = Profit	かもく 科目 = (School) subject	かがく 科学 = Science	きょうかしょ 教科書 = Textbook

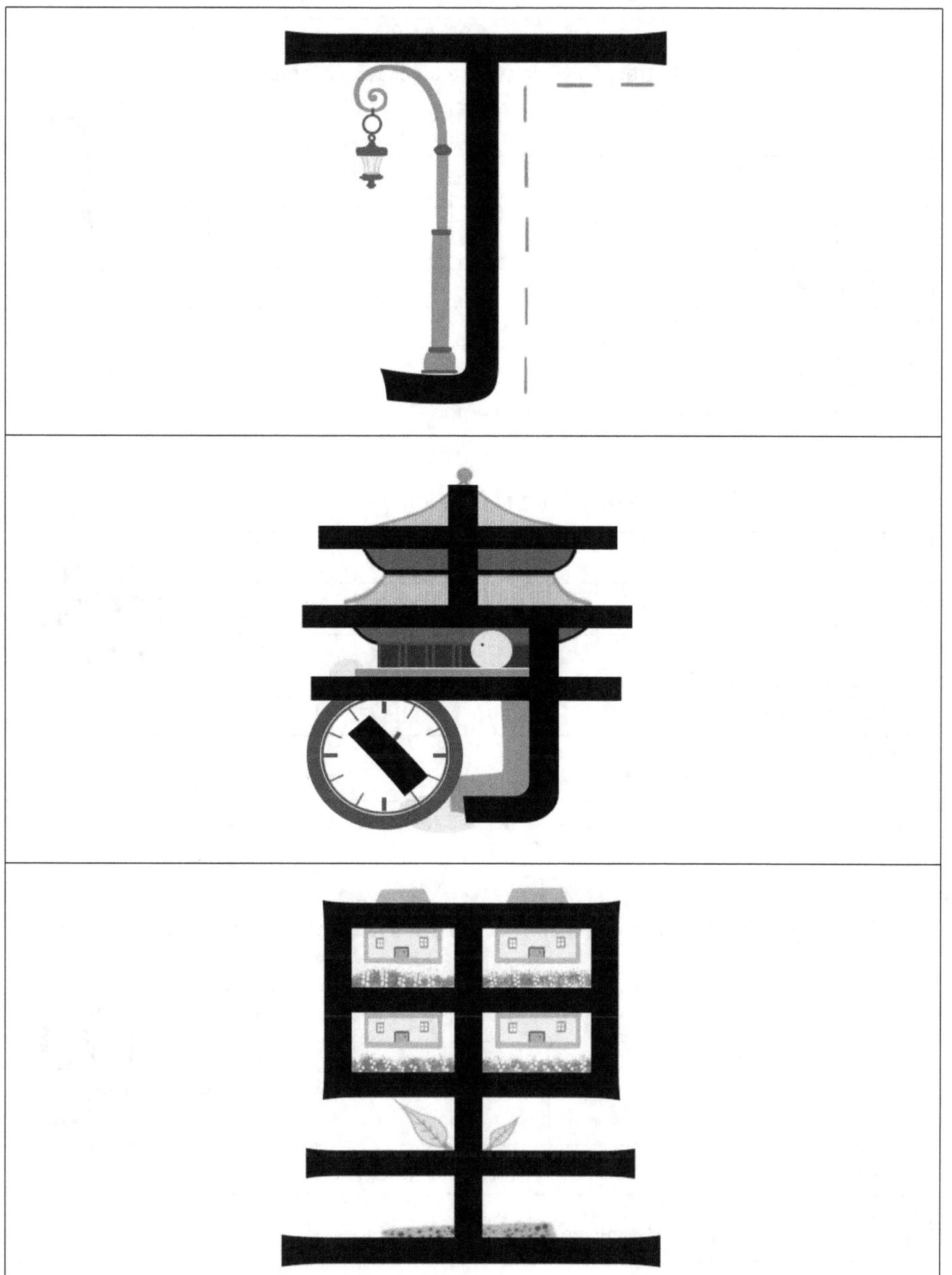

丁 STREET, WARD

"A street (丁) in a square block with a lamp"

SIMILAR KANJI	ON (テイ)
打 = Hit 灯 = Lamp	ていねい 丁寧 = Polite

* The original kanji was a nail that when pounded down it would look like a square block.

寺 TEMPLE

"A temple (寺) for Buddhist monks"

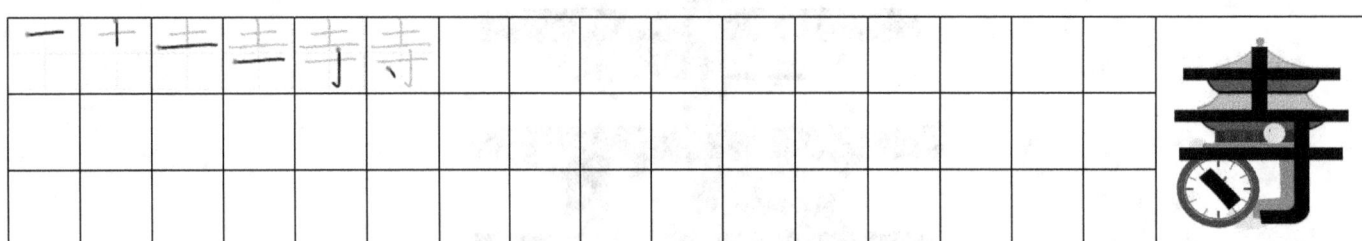

SIMILAR KANJI	Kun (てら)
侍 = Samurai 待 = Wait	てら 寺 = Temple

* The original kanji had a foot and a hand. It meant to work in the government. As monks started staying in government buildings, the kanji's meaning changed to temple.

里 VILLAGE

"The village (里) shares among themselves the soil (土) and the rice paddies (田) for sustainment"

SIMILAR KANJI	Kun (さと)
黒 = Black 理 = Logic	ふるさと 古里 = Home town, birthplace, old village

CHAPTER 8: ABSTRACT

神	福	礼	貯	相	観
145	146	147	148	149	150
組	給	級	利	列	残
151	152	153	154	155	156
戦	式	差	由	位	氏
157	158	159	160	161	162
役	徒	欠	順	類	共
163	164	165	166	167	168
令	命	的	協	芸	形
169	170	171	172	173	174
量	予	祭	実	害	関
175	176	177	178	179	180

神

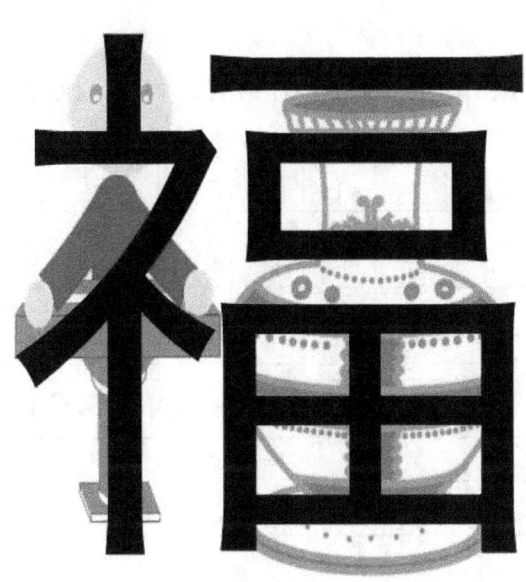

福

礼

神 GODS, MIND

"Praying to the god (神) of lighting (申) at the altar (ネ)"

SIMILAR KANJI	ON (シン)		Kun (かみ)
伸 = Expand	しんけい 神経 = Nerve, sensitivity じんじゃ 神社 = Shinto shrine	せいしん 精神 = Mind, soul	かみ 神 = God

*Lighting in the sky was considered God speaking. This is the reason why the kanji 申 means "to say". Yet as a radical, it still means lighting.

福 BLESSING, WEALTH

"Let's offer a wine container (畐) at the altar (ネ) and pray for blessings (福)"

SIMILAR KANJI	ON (フク)
副 = Assistant 幅 = Hanging scroll	こうふく 幸福 = Blessedness

礼 CEREMONY, BOW

"You must bend (乚) at the altar (ネ) during the ceremony (礼) to worship the gods"

SIMILAR KANJI	ON (レイ)	
乱 = Riot 乳 = Milk	れい 礼 = Expression of gratitude	れいぎ 礼儀 = Manners, courtesy

貯

相

觀

貯 SAVINGS, STORE

"Keep your savings (貯) of money (貝) protected under the roof (宀) of a bank instead of spending it out in the streets (丁)"

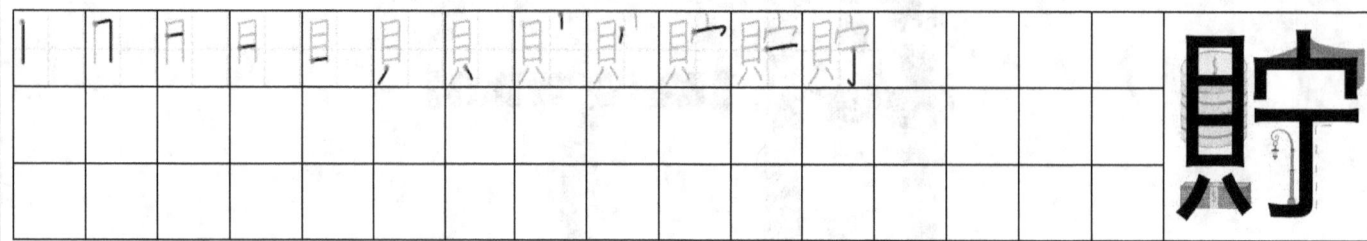

SIMILAR KANJI	ON (チョ)
財 = Wealth	ちょきん 貯金 = (Bank) Savings, putting money aside

*The original kanji was a cowrie inside a box, as a meaning of protecting valuable things.

相 MUTUAL, EACH OTHER

"The eye (目) looks at the tree (木) and realizes how much they need each other (相)"

SIMILAR KANJI	ON (ソウ、ショウ)		Kun (あい)
想 = Thought 箱 = Box	そうとう 相当 = Suitable そうぞく 相続 = Succession	しゅしょう 首相 = Prime minister そうだん 相談 = Consultation	あいて 相手 = Partner

観 OUTLOOK, APPEARANCE

"I carefully look (見) at the appearance (観) of small birds (隹) to find inspiration"

SIMILAR KANJI	ON (カン)		Kun (み)
勧 = Persuade 現 = Present	かんきゃく 観客 = Spectator かんさつ 観察 = Observation	かんこう 観光 = Sightseeing	み 観る = To see, to watch

組 CLASS, CREW, SET

"This set (組) of yarns (糸) were left by our ancestors (且) as a family symbol"

SIMILAR KANJI	Kun (くみ、く)	
祖 = Ancestor 租 = Tariff	ばんぐみ 番 組 = TV or radio program くみあい 組 合 = Association	くみ 組 = Class, group, team く 組む = To put together

給 SALARY, WAGE

"This wage (給) will fit (合) the quantity of the yarn (糸) you can produce"

SIMILAR KANJI	ON (キュウ)		
合 = Fit 拾 = Pick up	きゅうりょう 給 料 = Salary	きょうきゅう 供 給 = Supply	しきゅう 支 給 = Payment

*The kanji 合 is a container with a lid that fit each other well. This is the reason behind the meaning to fit.

級 CLASS, RANK

"Back in the old days, reaching (及) out for the correct threads (糸) and ranking (級) them for the loom was essential"

SIMILAR KANJI	ON (キュウ)
及 = Reach out 吸 = Inhale	きゅう 級 = Class, grade

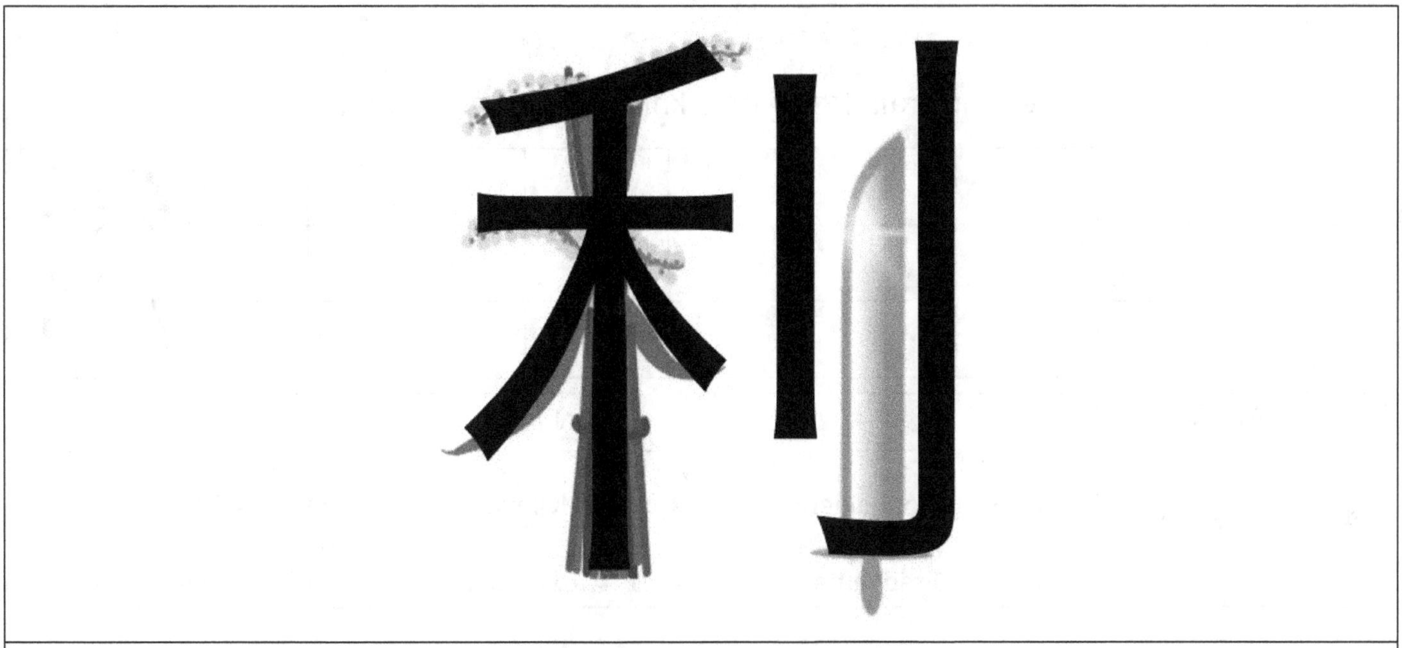

利

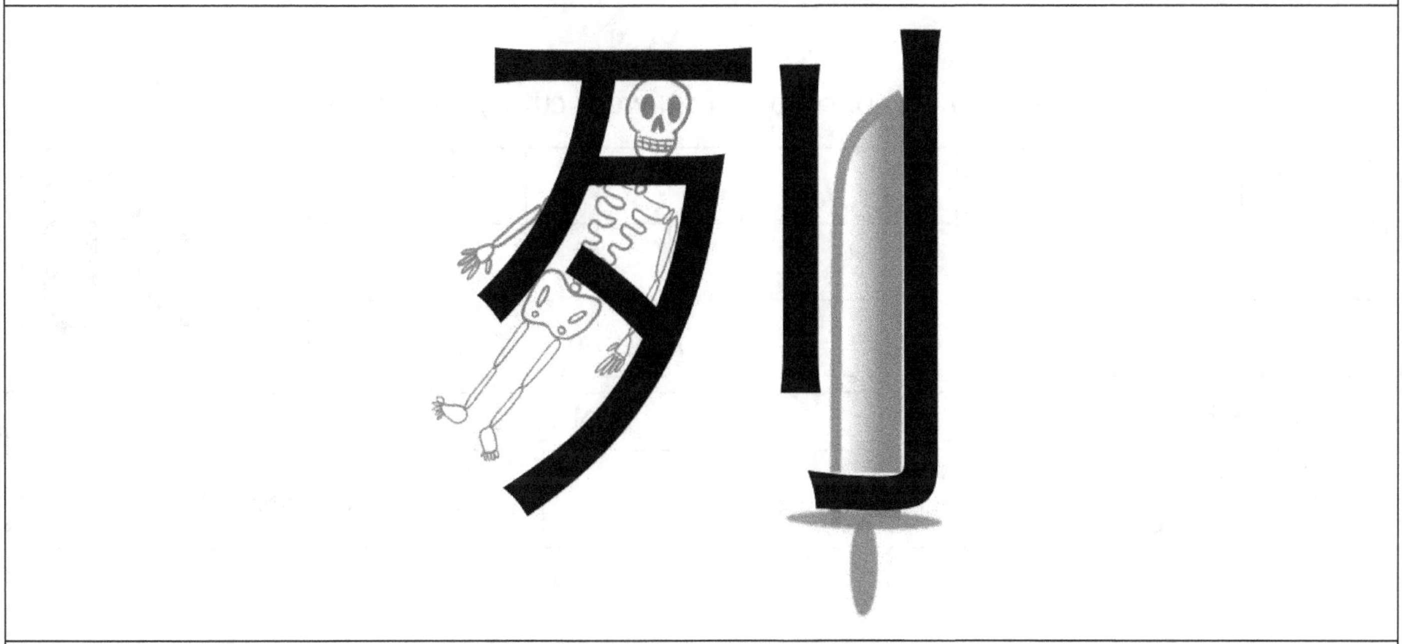

列

残

利 PROFIT, ADVANTAGE

"We reap grain (禾) with a knife (刂) for profit (利)"

SIMILAR KANJI	ON (リ)		
刈 = Reap 科 = Department	べんり 便利 = Convenient ふり 不利 = Disadvantage	けんり 権利 = Privilege ゆうり 有利 = Advantageous	りえき 利益 = Profits りこう 利口 = Clever

列 FILE, ROW

"That row (列) of corpses (歹) were cut by knife (刂)"

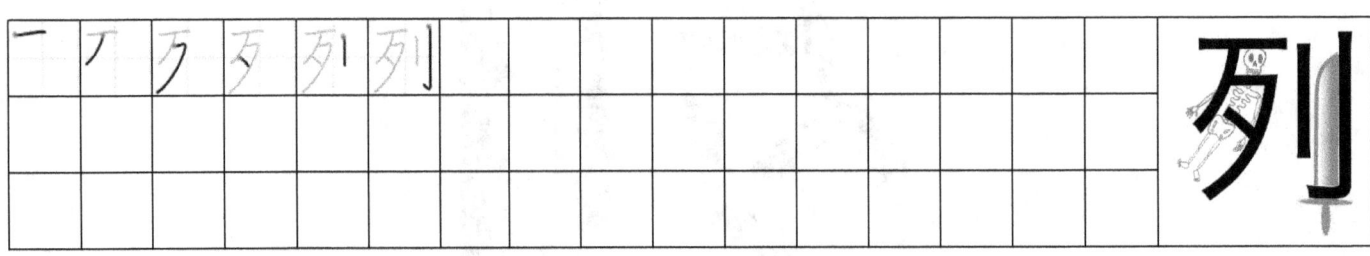

SIMILAR KANJI	ON (レツ)	
例 = Example 烈 = Ardent, violent	れつ 列 = Queue, row, line	れっしゃ 列車 = Train (ordinary)

残 REMAINS, LEFTOVER

"Removing the corpse (歹) remains (残) with a halberd (戈)"

SIMILAR KANJI	ON (ザン)	Kun (のこ)
浅 = Shallow 銭 = Coin	ざんねん 残念 = Regrettable	のこ 残り = Remnant のこ 残す = To leave (behind, over)

戦 WAR, BATTLE, MATCH

"Let's win the war (戦) by holding a single (単) halberd (戈)"

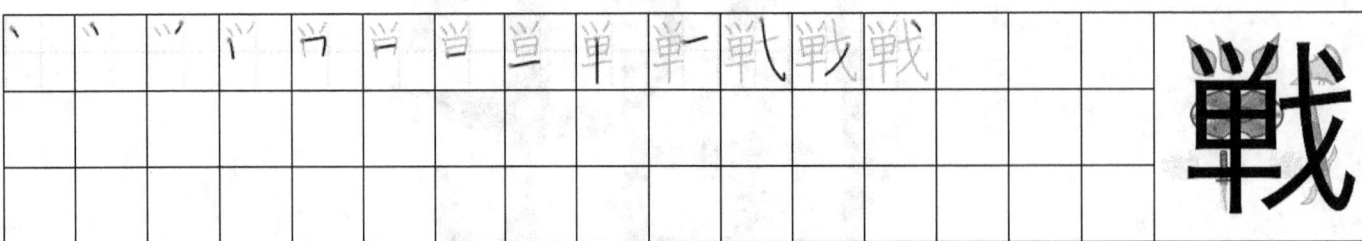

SIMILAR KANJI	ON (セン)	
単 = Simple, single 獣 = Beast	せんそう 戦争 = War	たいせん 対戦 = Great war, great battle

式 CEREMONY, SYSTEM

"Let's make some crafts (工) for the ceremony (式) using spikes (弋)"

SIMILAR KANJI	ON (シキ)	
試 = Test 弐 = Second	しき 式 = Equation, ceremony	せいしき 正式 = Due form, formality

差 DISTICTION, DIFFERENCE

"There's a difference (差) in making crafts (工) using sheep (羊) wool instead of polyester"

SIMILAR KANJI	ON (サ)	Kun (さ)
着 = Wear 看 = Watch over	こうさてん 交差点 = Intersection さべつ 差別 = Discrimination	さ 差 = Difference さ 差す = To raise, to shine

*The meaning of this kanji was originally "to rub hands" and it came from rubbing grains inside hands.

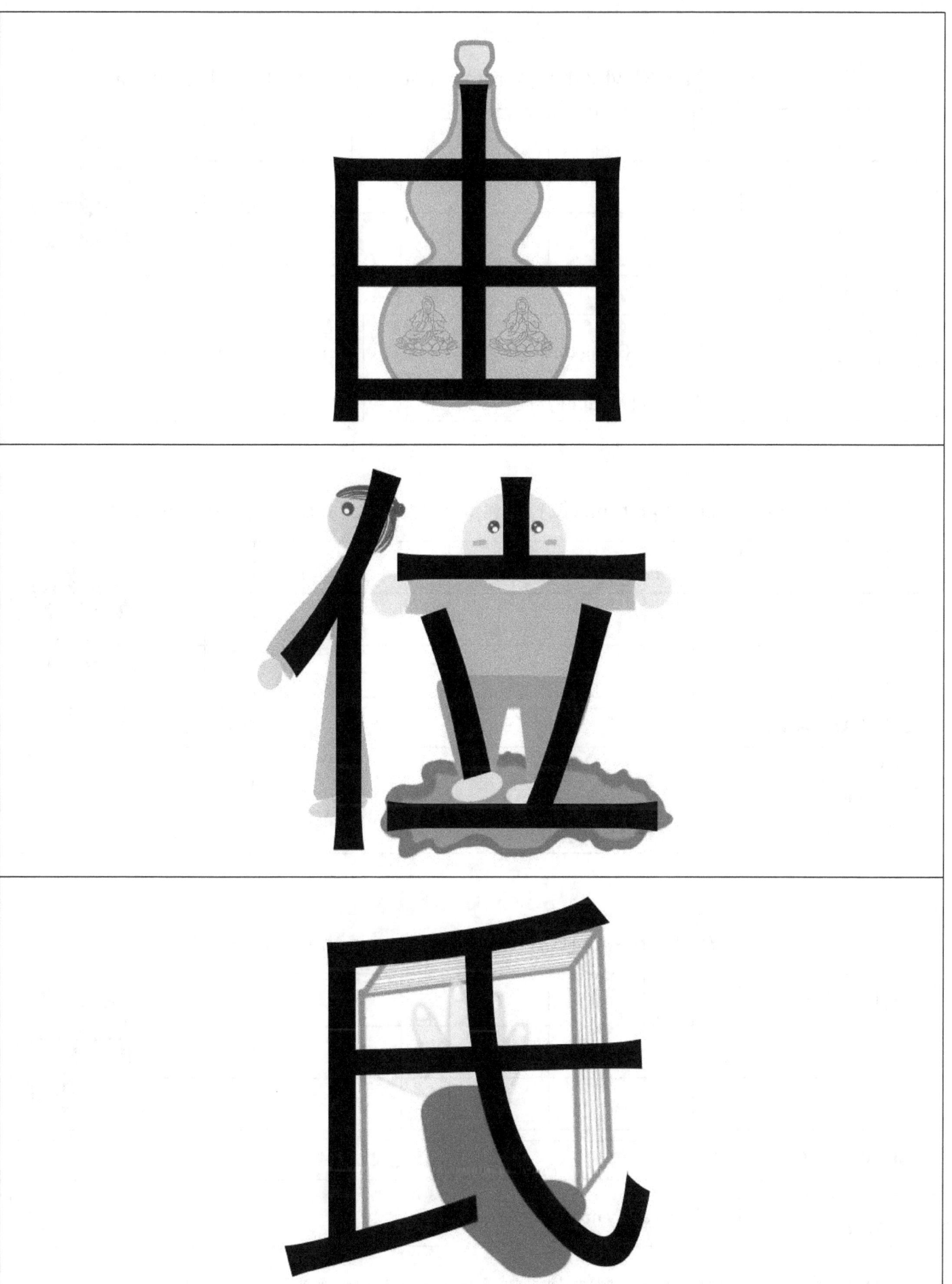

由 A REASON

"There is a reason (由) why the gourd became empty, and I need to find out"

SIMILAR KANJI	ON (ユ、ユウ)	
宙 = Air, space 曲 = Music, bend	けいゆ 経由 = Going through じゆう 自由 = Freedom	ふじゆう 不自由 = Discomfort

位 RANK, GRADE, THRONE

"A person (イ) in a high rank (位) is responsible for standing up (立) for others"

SIMILAR KANJI	ON (イ)	Kun (くらい)
泣 = Cry 立 = Stand up	いち 位置 = Place, situation たんい 単位 = Unit, denomination	くらい 位 = Grade, rank, throne ちい 地位 = (Social) status

氏 SURNAME, CLAN

"Your surname (氏) must be written in the registry"

SIMILAR KANJI	ON (シ)
民 = People, nation 紙 = Paper	し 氏 = Family name

* There are multiple interpretations for its origin which include a totem signifying a clan, a root of a tree, and others.

役 DUTY, WAR

"I am holding a tool (殳) as part of my duty (役) of guarding the road (彳)"

SIMILAR KANJI	ON (ヤク)	
投 = Throw 段 = Stairs	やく 役 = Use, service, role やくた 役に立つ = To be helpful	やくわり 役割 = Part, duties

徒 ON FOOT, FUTILITY

"Running (走) or going on foot (徒) on this road (彳) while following my master's life path"

SIMILAR KANJI	ON (ト)
走 = Run 赴 = Proceed	せいと 生徒 = Pupil

欠 LACK, GAP

"The person (人) is lacking (欠) air"

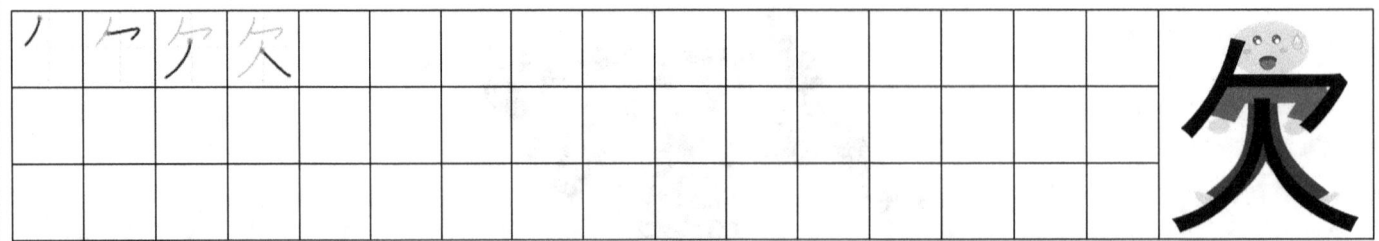

SIMILAR KANJI	ON (ケツ)		Kun (か)
吹 = Breath 次 = Next	けっかん 欠陥 = Defect, fault けっせき 欠席 = Absence	けってん 欠点 = Faults, defect	か 欠ける = To be lacking, to be broken

順

類

其

順 OBEY, ORDER, DOCILITY

"While watching the flow of the river (川), I put some order (順) to the thoughts in my head (頁)"

SIMILAR KANJI	ON (ジュン)		
訓 = Instruction 傾 = Lean	じゅん 順 = Order	じゅんちょう 順調 = Favorable	じゅんばん 順番 = Turn (in line)

類 SORT, KIND

"The master head (頁) of the temple offers the largest (大) and best kind (類) of grains of rice (米) to the gods"

SIMILAR KANJI	ON (ルイ)		
数 = Number	しゅるい 種類 = Variety, kind	しょるい 書類 = Documents	じんるい 人類 = Mankind

*The original kanji had the radical for dog (犬) instead of big (大).

共 TOGETHER, BOTH

"The two hands are making something together (共)"

SIMILAR KANJI	ON (キョウ)	Kun (とも)
供 = Submit 洪 = Flood	きょうつう 共通 = Common, shared きょうどう 共同 = Cooperation	とも 共に = Together, jointly

令 ORDER, LAW

"Kneel (卩) down when inside your master's roof (亼) and follow his orders (令)"

SIMILAR KANJI	ON (レイ)
今 = Now 命 = Fate, life	めいれい 命令 = Order, command

命 FATE, LIFE

"In life (命) follow orders (令) coming from the mouths (口) of your superiors"

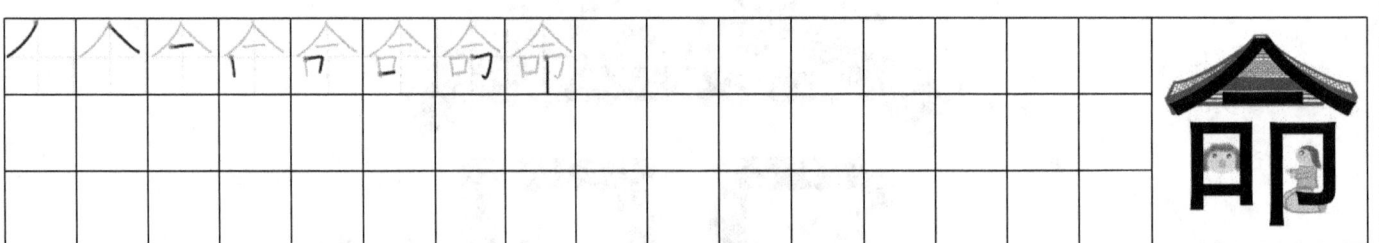

SIMILAR KANJI	ON (メイ)	Kun (いのち)
令 = Order, law 含 = Contain	せいめい 生命 = Life, existence めい 命じる = To order	めいれい 命令 = Order, command いっしょうけんめい 一生懸命 = Very hard	いのち 命 = Life

的 MARK, TARGET

"Put a mark (的) on the spoon (勺) with the white (白) candle light"

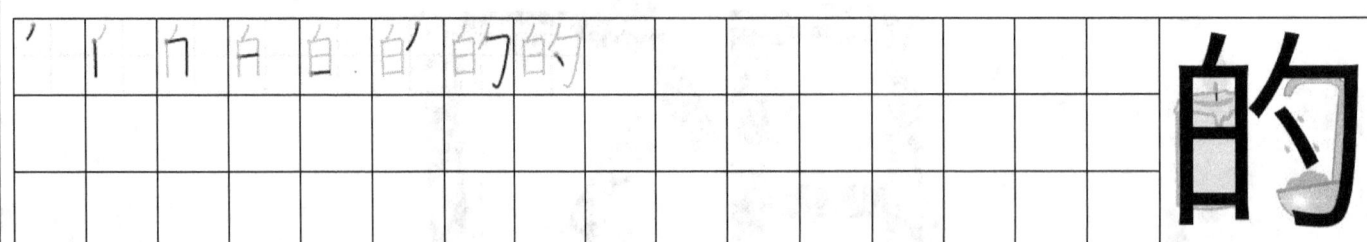

SIMILAR KANJI	ON (テキ)
約 = Promise 釣 = Angling	せっきょくてき 積極的 = Positive	もくてき 目的 = Purpose, goal

*The original Kanji had the radical sun instead of white. The sun would make something bright and therefore a precise target.

協

芸

形

協 COOPERATION

"This is a team of ten (十) strong (力) people that rely on cooperation (協) to get the job done"

SIMILAR KANJI	ON (キョウ)
脅 = Threaten	きょうりょく 協　力 = Cooperation, collaboration

芸 TECHNIQUE, ART

"Cloud (云) pruning is a Japanese technique (芸) to train trees and certain plants (艹) into shapes resembling clouds"

SIMILAR KANJI	ON (ゲイ)
会 = Meeting 伝 = Transmit	げいじゅつ 芸　術 = (Fine) art, the arts

* The original kanji looked different (藝) and meant "to have the skills to take care of a plant".

形 SHAPE, FORM

"When I see the two poles (开) in front of the barber shop, I go inside to change the shape (形) of my hair (彡)"

SIMILAR KANJI	ON (ギョウ)	Kun (かたち)
刑 = Punish 影 = Shadow	にんぎょう 人　形 = Doll, puppet	かたち 形 = Shape, form

量 QUANTITY, MEASURE, AMOUNT

"What quantity (量) of rice (田) grain was gathered by dawn (旦) in the village (里)?"

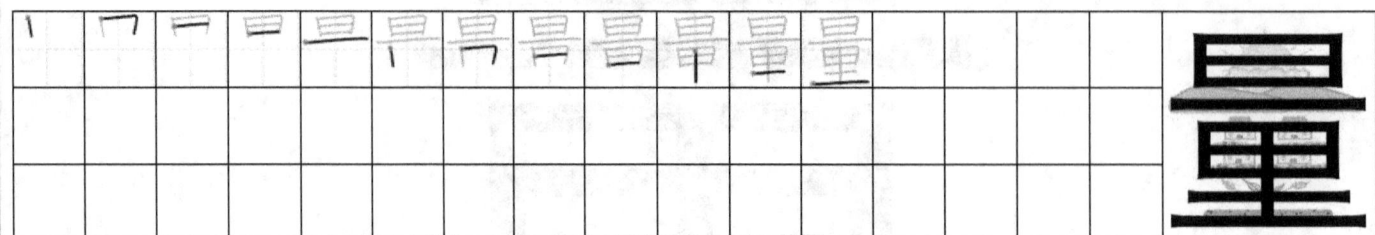

SIMILAR KANJI	ON (リョウ)
童 = Juvenile 里 = Village	りょう 量 = Quantity, amount

予 BEFOREHAND, MYSELF

"I get everything ready beforehand (予) to feel everything is under control"

SIMILAR KANJI	ON (ヨ)		
子 = Child 矛 = Halberd	よほう 予報 = Prediction よそく 予測 = Estimation	よてい 予定 = Arrangement よやく 予約 = Reservation	よき 予期 = Forecast よさん 予算 = Budget

祭 RITUAL, CELEBRATE

"The ritual (祭) starts by making an offering of meat (月) on the altar (示)"

SIMILAR KANJI	Kun (まつり)
察 = Judge, guess 発 = Departure	まつり 祭 = Festival

実 REALITY, TRUTH

"The big (大) samurai (士) under the roof (宀) fights for truth (実) and justice"

SIMILAR KANJI	ON (ジツ)		
美 = Beautiful 寒 = Cold	かくじつ 確 実 = Certainty じっけん 実 験 = Experiment	げんじつ 現 実 = Reality じつげん 実 現 = Realization	じじつ 事 実 = Fact, truth じっこう 実 行 = Execution

* The original kanji was 實 and it was related to wealth.

害 HARM, INJURY

"A mouth (口) that talks indiscriminately under their own roof (宀), causes more harm (害) than a poisonous plant (丰)"

SIMILAR KANJI	ON (ガイ)		
毒 = Poison 割 = Proportion	がい 害 = Injury	しょうがい 障 害 = Obstacle	ひがい 被 害 = Damage, harm

関 CONNECTION, GATEWAY

"The main gateway (関) is closed securely with bolts"

SIMILAR KANJI	ON (カン)		
開 = Open 閑 = Leisure	げんかん 玄 関 = Entry hall かん 関 する = To concern	かんしん 関 心 = Concern, interest きかん 機 関 = Engine, institution	かんれん 関 連 = Relation

* The element for bolts was  but it was simplified into 关

CHAPTER 9: FEELINGS

愛	恋	想	念	感	信
181	182	183	184	185	186
功	勇	希	幸	栄	和
187	188	189	190	191	192
敗					
193					

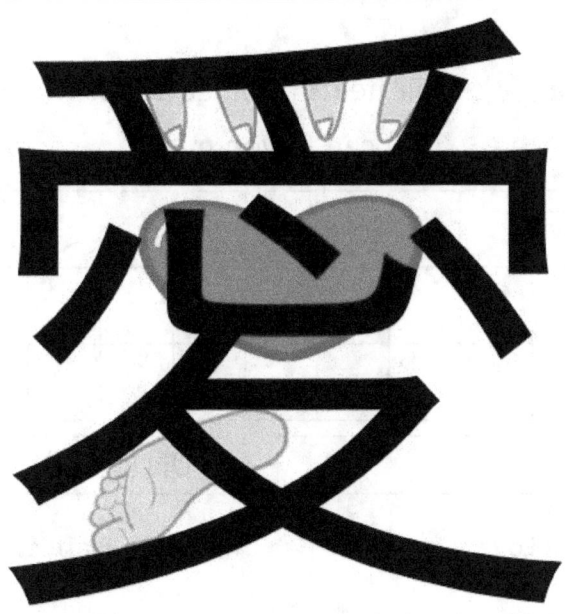

愛 LOVE, AFFECTION

"When someone is in love (愛), their heart (心) beats fast while their hands (爫) and feet (夂) can't even move"

SIMILAR KANJI	ON (アイ)
受 = Accept 憂 = Melancholy	あい 愛 = Love あいじょう 愛情 = Love, affection あい 愛する = To love

恋 ROMANCE, IN LOVE

"This person's heart (心) is once again deep in love (恋)"

SIMILAR KANJI	Kun (こい)
変 = Strange	こい 恋 = Love, tender

想 CONCEPT, THINK, THOUGHT

"The thought (想) in our hearts (心) should have mutual (相) respect towards nature"

SIMILAR KANJI	ON (ソウ)
箱 = Box 相 = Mutual	しそう 思想 = Thought, idea りそう 理想 = Idea	そうぞう 想像 = Imagination, guess れんそう 連想 = Suggestion

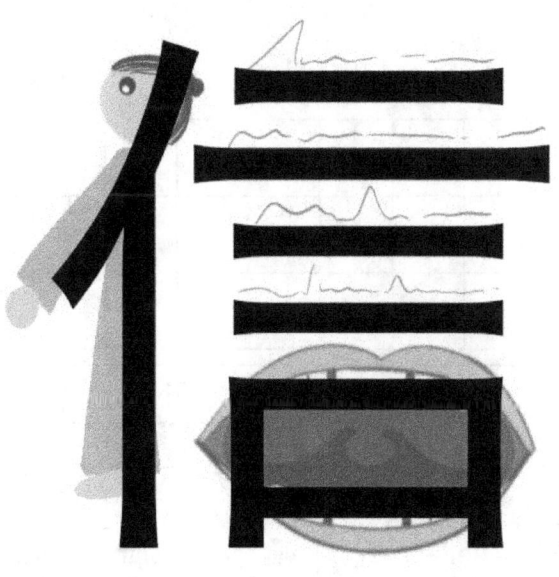

念 WISH, DESIRE

"Something that you've kept in your heart (心) until now (今) that is probably your biggest desire (念)"

SIMILAR KANJI	ON (ネン)	
今 = Now 含 = Contain	きねん 記念 = Commemoration	ざんねん 残念 = Regrettable

感 EMOTION, FEELING

"Watch your mouth (口) when you have multiple emotions (感) in your heart (心)"

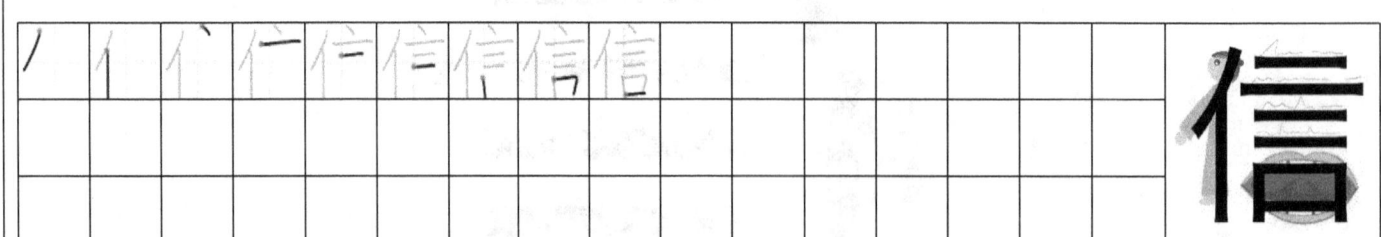

SIMILAR KANJI	ON (カン)		
惑 = Delusion 憾 = Remorse	かんかく 感覚 = Sensation かんじょう 感情 = Emotion(s)	かん 感じ = Feeling かん 感じる = To feel	かんしゃ 感謝 = Thanks かんしん 感心 = Admiration

信 FAITH, TRUST

"It is important to trust (信) a person's (亻) words (言)"

SIMILAR KANJI	ON (シン)		
言 = Say	しんこう 信仰 = Belief しんらい 信頼 = Reliance	しんごう 信号 = Traffic lights つうしん 通信 = Signal, news	しん 信じる = To believe しんよう 信用 = Confidence

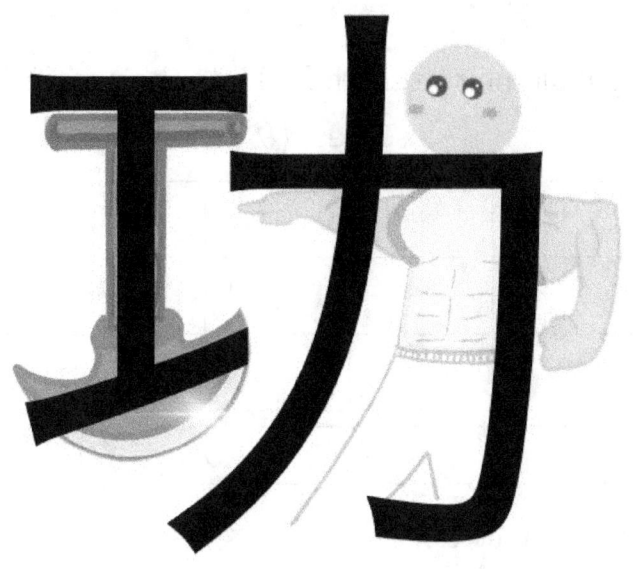

功

勇

希

功 ACHIEVEMENT, MERITS

"People who put all their strength (力) into their crafts (工) can reach success (功)"

SIMILAR KANJI	ON (コウ)
切 = Cut 初 = First time	せいこう 成功 = Success, hit

勇 COURAGE, BRAVERY

"The strong (力) man passes through (甬) life with courage (勇)"

SIMILAR KANJI	ON (ユウ)
男 = Male 湧 = Ferment	ゆうき 勇気 = Courage

希 HOPE, RARE

"The cross (乂) bow on this cloth (巾) signifies hope (希)"

SIMILAR KANJI	ON (キ)
布 = Clothe 怖 = Dreadful	きぼう 希望 = Hope, wish

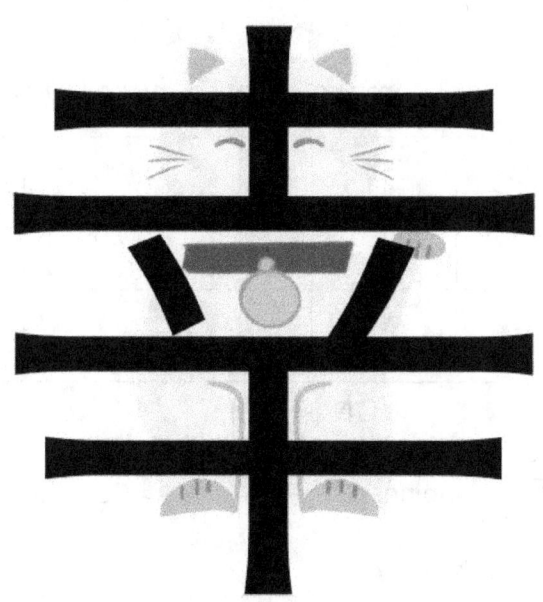

幸 HAPPINESS, BLESSING

"The fortune cat seems to carry so much happiness (幸)"

SIMILAR KANJI	ON (コウ)		Kun (しあわ、さいわ)
辛 = Spicy 宰 = Superintend	こうふく 幸福 = Happiness ふこう 不幸 = Unhappiness	こううん 幸運 = Good luck, fortune	さいわ 幸い = Happiness しあわ 幸せ = Happiness

*The original kanji was the combination of the elements opposite + death = lucky to be alive.

栄 FLOURISH, PROSPERITY

"Setting a large open-air fire (火) by the big trees (木) signifies a celebration for our prosperity (栄)"

SIMILAR KANJI	ON (エイ)
床 = Bed 木 = Tree	えいよう 栄養 = Nutrition, nourishment

和 HARMONY, PEACE

"We can freely grow grains (禾) and feed mouths (口) when there's peace (和)"

SIMILAR KANJI	ON (ワ)
知 = Know 私 = I	へいわ 平和 = Peace, harmony

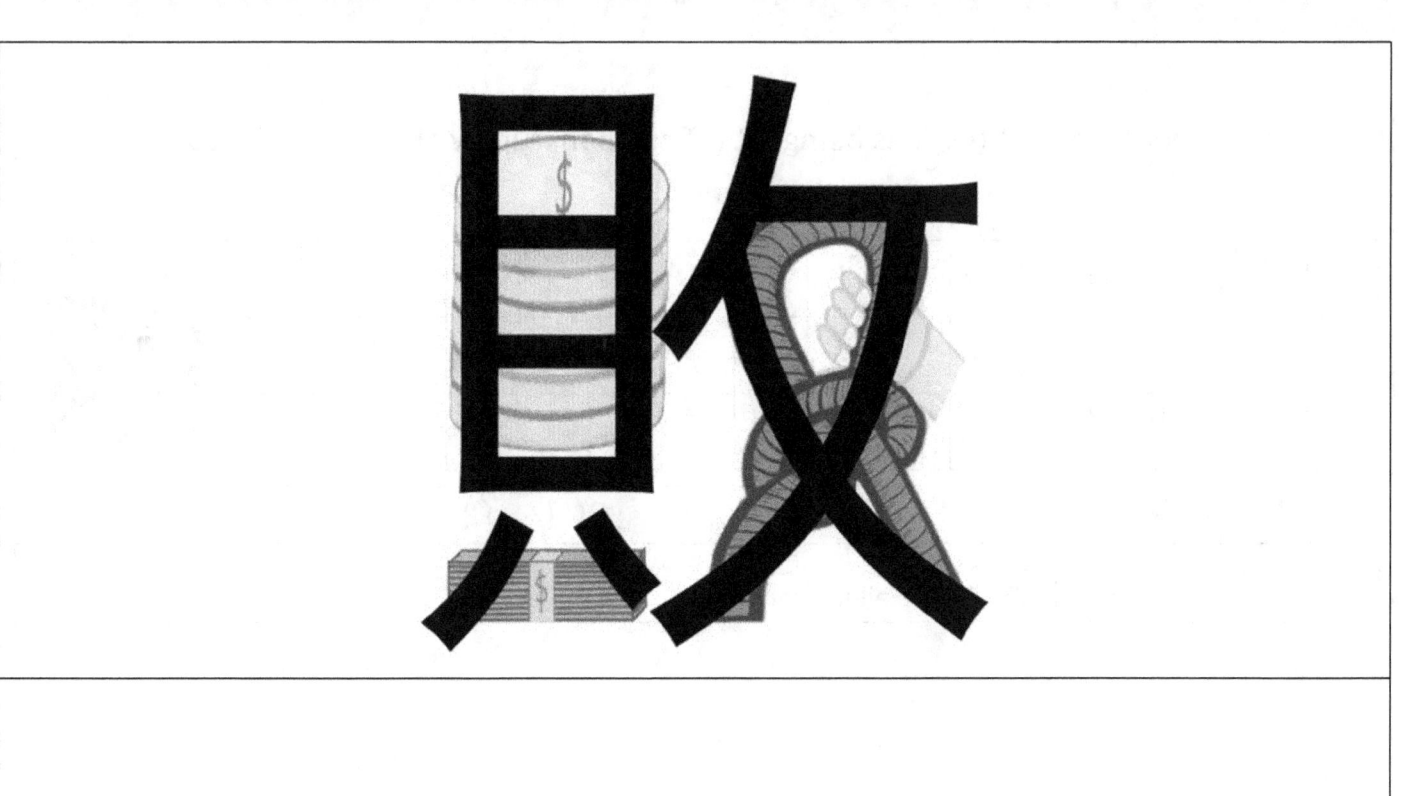

敗 FAILURE, DEFEAT

"What a defeat (敗) it is being hit (攵) by bankruptcy and losing all your money (貝)"

丨	冂	冃	月	貝	貝	貝'	貝/	敗	敗				

SIMILAR KANJI	ON (ハイ)
販 = Marketing	しっぱい 失 敗 = Failure, mistake

Yay! Only 168 more Kanji to go!

頑張ってください！

CHAPTER 10: ADJECTIVES

丸	才	良	悲	必	変
194	195	196	197	198	199
最	昭	温	浅	深	満
200	201	202	203	204	205
清	静	冷	速	苦	完
206	207	208	209	210	211
単	平	美	細	緑	黄
212	213	214	215	216	217
等	努	全	健	康	直
218	219	220	221	222	223

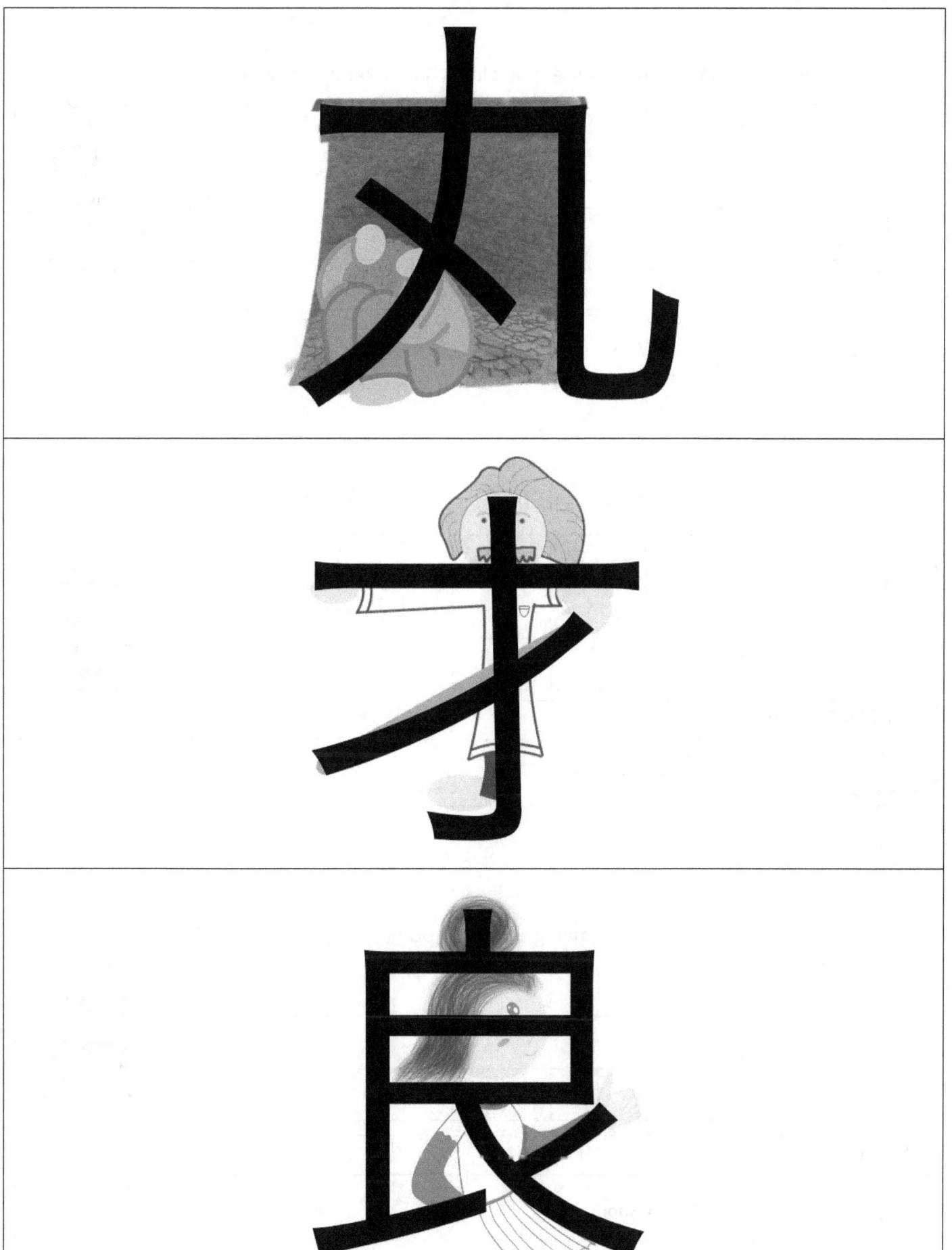

丸 ROUND, CURL UP

"Nine (九) people hide under the cliff while making a round (丸) shape"

SIMILAR KANJI	Kun (まる)	
九 = Nine 刃 = Blade	まる 丸い = Round	まる 丸 = Circle, full (month)

才 GENIUS, YEARS OLD

"Albert Einstein was a genius (才)"

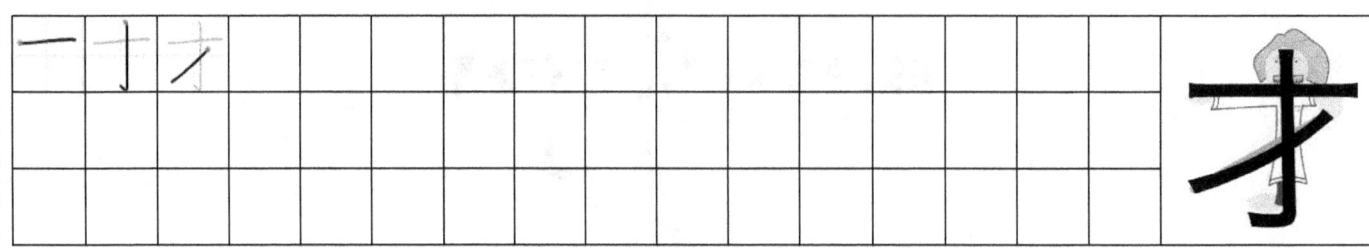

SIMILAR KANJI	ON (サイ)
丈 = Length 丁 = Street	さいのう 才能 = Talent

*The kanji originally was a seed sprouting.

良 GOOD, PLEASING

"The girl is giving us the good (良) to go sign"

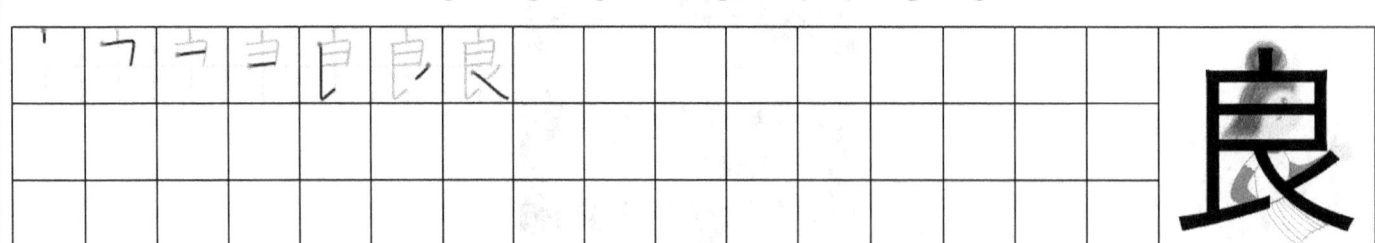

SIMILAR KANJI	Kun (よ)
娘 = Daughter 恨 = Regret	よ 良い = Good

* Multiple suggestions have been made to the origin of this kanji such as a pavilion or a meaning of beauty.

悲 GRIEVE, SAD

"The heart (心) feels sad (悲) after making a mistake (非) so I cover my eyes"

SIMILAR KANJI	ON (ヒ)	Kun (かな)
俳 = Actor 扉 = Front door	ひげき 悲劇 = Tragedy	かな 悲しむ = To be sad かな 悲しい = Sad

* Originally 非 were two opposing wings that never meant to be together and gave the meaning of "Not good".

必 CERTAIN, INEVITABLE

"It is inevitable (必) for a heart (心) to die when pierced by an arrow"

SIMILAR KANJI	ON (ヒツ)	Kun (かなら)
心 = Heart 泌 = Flow	ひっし 必死 = Inevitable death	かなら 必ずしも = (Not) always かなら 必ず = Certainly

*The original Kanji didn't have anything to do with the radical for heart 心, but it was more some sort of tool.

変 STRANGE, UNUSUAL

"That person's foot (夂) is once again (亦) moving strange (変)"

SIMILAR KANJI	ON (ヘン)		Kun (か)
恋 = In love	へんか 変化 = Change, variation へんこう 変更 = Change, modification	たいへん 大変 = Awful	か 変える = To change

最

昭

温

最 MOST, EXTREME

"Extreme (最) exposure to sun (日) is harmful, so always take (取) the shadow"

SIMILAR KANJI	ON (サイ)		Kun (もっと)
撮 = Take pictures 取 = Take, catch	さいちゅう 最中 = In the midst of さいてい 最低 = Least, worst	さいこう 最高 = Highest さいしゅう 最終 = Last, final	もっと 最も = Extremely

* The original meaning behind this kanji was long lost. It was used in the military as "offend and take away"

昭 SHINING, BRIGHT

"I've been summoned (召) to stand under the bright (昭) sun (日)"

SIMILAR KANJI	ON (ショウ)
沼 = Marsh, lake 照 = Illuminate	しょうわ 昭和 = Shouwa era (1926 – 1989)

温 WARM

"Sun (日) rays boil water (氵) inside this bowl (皿) and makes it warm (温)"

SIMILAR KANJI	ON (オン)		ODD (ぬる)
塩 = Salt 湿 = Damp	おんど 温度 = Temperature おんだん 温暖 = Warm	きおん 気温 = Temperature (air) たいおん 体温 = Temperature (body)	ぬる 温い = Luke warm

浅

深

満

浅 SHALLOW, SUPERFICIAL

"The water (氵) is so shallow (浅) that I can touch the bottom of it with my halberd (戈)"

SIMILAR KANJI	Kun (あさ)
残 = Leftover 銭 = Coin	あさ 浅い = Shallow

深 DEEP, INTENSIFY

"Searching for water (氵) deep (深) inside the cave (宀) and above the tree (木)"

SIMILAR KANJI	ON (シン)	Kun (ふか)
探 = Search 採 = Fetch	しんこく 深刻 = Serious	ふか 深い = Deep

* Originally instead of tree it was fire. The fire would be used as a light to search.

満 FULL, SATISFY

"Both (両) of my hands (廾) are full (満) of water (氵)"

SIMILAR KANJI	ON (マン)	Kun (み)
両 = Both 溝 = Gutter	ふまん 不満 = Displeasure, complaints まんぞく 満足 = Satisfaction	み 満ちる = To be full

清

静

冷

清 PURE, PURIFY

"A pure (清) light blue (青) water (氵) refreshes the night"

SIMILAR KANJI
- 情 = Emotion
- 晴 = Clear up

ON (セイ)
- せいけつ
- 清潔 = Clean

静 QUIET

"After disputes (争), all that is left is a quiet (静) blue (青) sky"

SIMILAR KANJI
- 浄 = Clean, purify
- 争 = Dispute

ON (セイ)
- れいせい
- 冷静 = Calm, composure

Kun (しず)
- しず
- 静か = Quiet

冷 COLD, CHILL

"She became cold (冷) as ice (冫) when she heard the new military order (令)"

SIMILAR KANJI
- 今 = Now
- 令 = Order

ON (レイ)
- れいぞうこ
- 冷蔵庫 = Refrigerator
- れいせい
- 冷静 = Calm, composure
- れいぼう
- 冷房 = Air conditioning

Kun (つめ、ひ)
- つめ
- 冷たい = Cold to the touch
- ひ
- 冷える = To grow cold

速 QUICK, FAST

"The bundles (束) of wood must be taken to the road (辶) fast (速)"

SIMILAR KANJI	ON (ソク)	Kun (はや)
束 = Bundle 連 = Take along	きゅうそく 急速 = Rapid こうそく 高速 = High speed	そくど 速度 = Speed	はや 速い = Quick

苦 SUFFERING, BITTER

"The plants (艹) that surround these old (古) graves are bitter (苦)"

SIMILAR KANJI	ON (ク)	Kun (くる、にが)	
若 = Young 古 = Old	くろう 苦労 = Troubles くつう 苦痛 = Pain, agony	くる 苦しい = Painful くる 苦しむ = To suffer	にがて 苦手 = Poor (at) にが 苦い = Bitter

完 PERFECT, COMPLETION

"The basis (元) to having the perfect (完) life starts with a roof (宀) as shelter for you and your family"

SIMILAR KANJI	ON (カン)		
元 = Origin 売 = Sell	かんせい 完成 = Perfection	かんぜん 完全 = Perfect	かんりょう 完了 = Completion

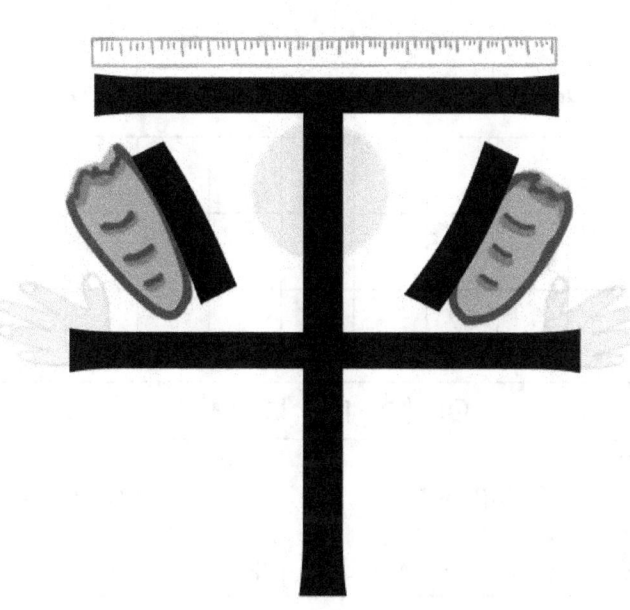

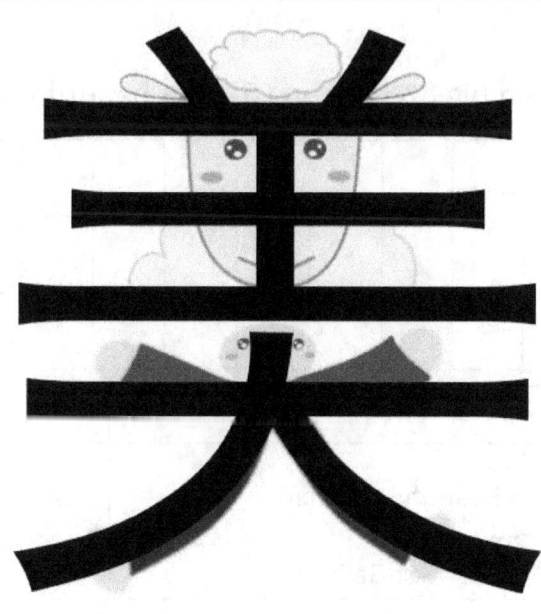

単 SIMPLE, SINGLE

"A simple (単) way to win this battle is by having ten (十) men with shields (甲)"

SIMILAR KANJI	ON (タン)		
果 = Fruit 戦 = War	たんい 単位 = Unit, denomination たんじゅん 単純 = Simplicity	たんご 単語 = Word, vocabulary たん 単なる = Mere, simple	かんたん 簡単 = Simple

平 EVEN, PEACE

"Ten (十) loaves of bread were cut even (平) for everyone"

SIMILAR KANJI	ON (ヘイ、ヒョウ)		Kun (たい)
半 = Half 末 = End	ふへい 不平 = Complaint ちへいせん 地平線 = Horizon	へいきん 平均 = Equilibrium びょうどう 平等 = Equality	たい 平ら = Flat, level

美 BEAUTY, BEAUTIFUL

"A mature and big (大) sheep (羊) is a beautiful (美) animal"

SIMILAR KANJI	ON (ビ)	Kun (うつく)
実 = Truth 羊 = Sheep	びじん 美人 = Beautiful (woman) びじゅつかん 美術館 = Art Gallery	うつく 美しい = Beautiful

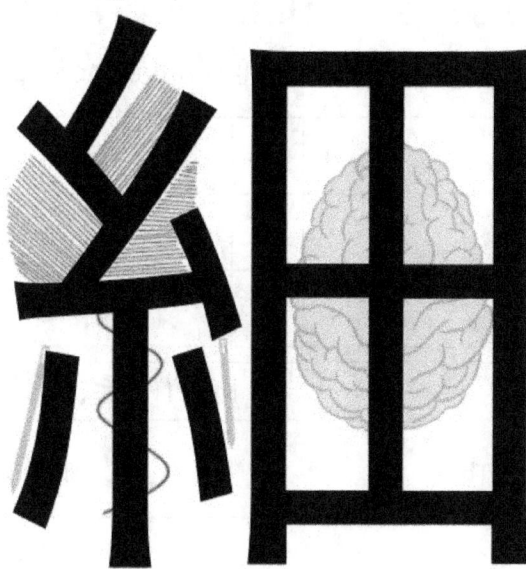

細 GET THIN, NARROW, PRECISE

"Working with yarn (糸) helps your brain (囟) have more precise (細) motor skills"

く	幺	幺	乡	糸	糸	糸	紅	細	細	細			

SIMILAR KANJI	Kun (ほそ、こま)	
畑 = Farm, field 神 = God	ほそ 細 い = Thin	こま 細 かい = Small, fine, trivial

* Originally the radical for brain started as 囟. In kanjis like this one it looks more like 田. Then it evolved to 凶.

緑 GREEN

"Green (緑) dies are obtained from leaves and were used to dye yarn (糸)"

く	幺	幺	乡	糸	糸	糸	紀	紀	紆	紵	緑	緑	

SIMILAR KANJI	Kun (みどり)
録 = Record 線 = Line	みどり 緑 = Green

黄 YELLOW

"Both hands together (共) hold a yellow (黄) jade"

一	十	廾	井	䒑	芇	苗	苗	黄	黄				

SIMILAR KANJI	Kun (き)	
横 = Sideways 演 = Performance	きいろ 黄 色 = Yellow	きいろ 黄 色 い = Yellow

等 ETC., EQUAL, CLASS

"The two bamboo (⺮) stems in the temple (寺) are of equal (等) length"

SIMILAR KANJI	ON (トウ)		Kun (ひと、など、ら)	
供 = Submit 洪 = Flood	じょうとう 上等 = Superiority びょうどう 平等 = Equality		など 等 = Etc. ひと 等しい = Equal	かれら 彼等 = They (usually male)

努 TOIL, DILIGENT

"The slave (奴) uses all her strength (力) to be very diligent (努) in her work"

SIMILAR KANJI	ON (ド)
奴 = Guy 怒 = Angry	どりょく 努力 = Effort, endeavor

全 WHOLE, ENTIRE

"The king (王) must help the entire (全) nation"

SIMILAR KANJI	ON (ゼン)		Kun (すべ)
金 = Gold 会 = Meet	ぜんぶ 全部 = All ぜんいん 全員 = All members	かんぜん 完全 = Completeness ぜんこく 全国 = Country-wide	すべ 全て = All, the whole

健 HEALTHY, STRENGTH

"Every person (亻) should build (建) good habits to stay healthy (健)"

SIMILAR KANJI	ON (ケン)
建 = Build 鍵 = Key	けんこう 健 康 = Health

康 EASE, PEACE

"The hand (ヨ) digs for clean water (水) under the tent (广) to provide everyone a healthy (康) life"

SIMILAR KANJI	ON (コウ)
庸 = Ordinary 逮 = Apprehend	けんこう 健 康 = Health

* Originally it had the element of rice instead of water.

直 STRAIGHT, HONESTY

"There is a straight (直) arrow tattoo above his eye"

SIMILAR KANJI	ON (ジキ、チョク)		Kun (ただ、す、なお)	
値 = Price 植 = To plant	じき 直 に = Immediately しょうじき 正 直 = Honesty	じき 直 = In a moment ちょくせつ 直 接 = Direct	ただ 直 ちに = At once ま す 真っ直ぐ = Upright	なお 直 す = To fix

CHAPTER 11: POSITION + TIME

央	仲	側	内	周	表
224	225	226	227	228	229
末	横	秒	反	歴	史
230	231	232	233	234	235
次	辺	対	昔	昨	期
236	237	238	239	240	241
囲	底	紀			
242	243	244			

央 CENTER, MIDDLE

"This person (イ) is in the middle of the world (央)"

ノ	ワ	ロ	中	央							

SIMILAR KANJI
映 = Reflect
英 = England

ON (オウ)
ちゅうおう
中央 = Center, middle

*This kanji was originally a person carrying a yoke.

仲 GO-BETWEEN, RELATIONSHIP

"That person (イ) acts as a go-between (仲) to get in the middle (中) of issues and work them out"

ノ	イ	イ	化	仁	仲						

SIMILAR KANJI
中 = Middle
沖 = Open sea

Kun (なか)
なか
仲 = Relation, relationship

なかま
仲間 = Fellow, colleague

側 SIDE, OPPOSE

"That person (イ) has a shellfish (貝) and a knife (刂) on his right-hand side (側)"

ノ	イ	イ	们	佀	佀	但	俱	俱	側	側	

SIMILAR KANJI
則 = Rule
測 = Fathom

Kun (そば)
そば
側 = Side, near, beside

内 INSIDE, WITHIN

"The person (人) is inside (内) an enclosure (冂)"

SIMILAR KANJI	ON (ナイ)		Kun (うち)
肉 = Meat 囚 = Captured	ないよう 内 容 = Subject, contents あんない 案 内 = Information, guidance	いない 以 内 = Within かない 家 内 = (My) wife	うち 内 = Inside, within

周 CIRCUMFERENCE, LAP

"We measure the circumference (周) of the plants (土) to put an enclosure (冂) around them. Then let them grow to feed many mouths (口)"

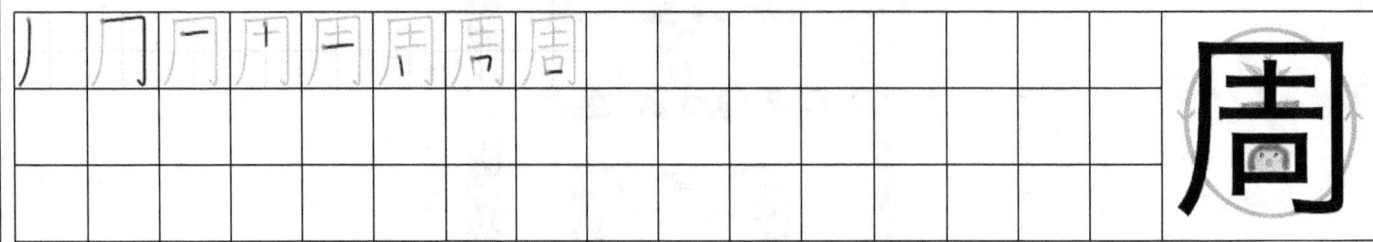

SIMILAR KANJI	ON (シュウ)	Kun (まわ)
週 = Week 調 = Tune	しゅうい 周 囲 = Surroundings, circumference	まわ 周 り = Surroundings, girth

表 SURFACE, TABLE

"There is hair (毛) stuck on the surface (表) of this garment (衣)"

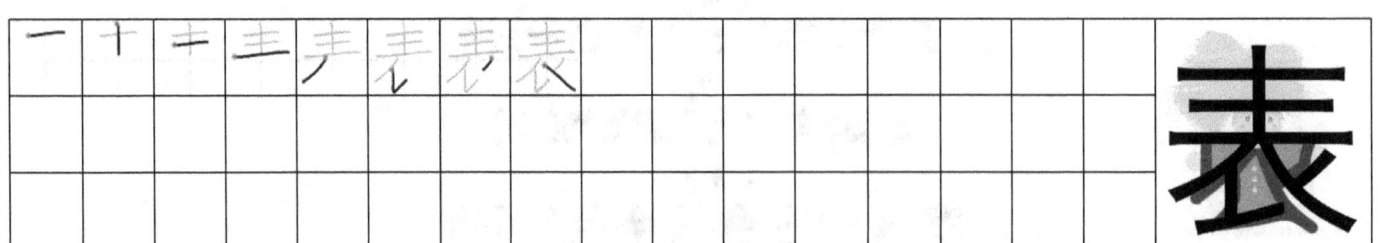

SIMILAR KANJI	ON (ヒョウ)		Kun (あらわ、おもて)
麦 = Wheat 裏 = Back	だいひょう 代 表 = Representative はっぴょう 発 表 = Announcement	ひょうげん 表 現 = Expression ひょう 表 = Chart, list	あらわ 表 す = To represent おもて 表 = Surface

末

横

秒

末 END

"If you see a bulge on a tree (木), it might be the end (末) of its growth"

SIMILAR KANJI	ON (マツ)	
未 = Not yet 夫 = Husband	そまつ 粗末 = Crude, rough	まつ 末 = The end of, powder

横 SIDEWAYS, HORIZONTAL

"I'll be using some wood (木) as a horizontal (横) base for the yellow (黄) jade"

SIMILAR KANJI	ON (オウ)	Kun (よこ)
演 = Performance 黄 = Yellow	おうだん 横断 = Crossing	よこ 横 = Beside, horizontal よこぎ 横切る = To traverse

秒 SECOND

"One second (秒) is as little (少) as one grain (禾)"

SIMILAR KANJI	ON (ビョウ)
少 = Little, few 砂 = Sand	びょう 秒 = Second

反 AGAINST, ANTI-
"The hand (又) is placed against (反) the cliff (厂) for support"

SIMILAR KANJI
板 = Board
坂 = Slope

ON (ハン)
いはん
違反 = Violation (of law), offense
はんたい
反対 = Opposition
はんこう
反抗 = Opposition, resistance

歴 CURRICULUM, PASSAGE OF TIME
"The passage of time (歴) never stops (止) and can be seen in the trees (木) during the seasons"

SIMILAR KANJI
暦 = Calendar

ON (レキ)
れきし
歴史 = History

*This kanji has a military origin. It signified how the army would move from one place to the other.

史 HISTORY, CHRONICLE
"The hand (ナ) holds a history (史) book right in the middle (中)"

SIMILAR KANJI
使 = Use
右 = Right

ON (シ)
れきし
歴史 = History

*There a several versions of what the hand was actually holding in this kanji. Yet, the assumption is that it was a historian keeping records.

次

辺

対

次 NEXT, ORDER

"The traveler yawns (欠), so at the next (次) two (二) stops, he will take a break"

SIMILAR KANJI	Kun (つぎ)	
吹 = Blow 欠 = Lack, yawn	つぎ 次 = Next, following	つぎつぎ 次々 = In succession

辺 BORDER, VICINITY

"I'm marking the borders (辺) of this road (辶) with a sword (刀)"

SIMILAR KANJI	ON (ヘン)	Kun (あた)
刀 = Sword 力 = Strength	へん 辺 = Area	あた 辺り = Vicinity, nearby

* The original kanji was 邊 and later simplified to 辺.

対 OPPOSITE, COMPARE

"Use different letters (文) to mark measurements (寸) in opposite directions (対)"

SIMILAR KANJI	ON (タイ)	
付 = Adhere 射 = Shoot	ぜったい 絶対 = Absolutely たいしょう 対象 = Target	はんたい 反対 = Opposition たい 対する = To face, to oppose

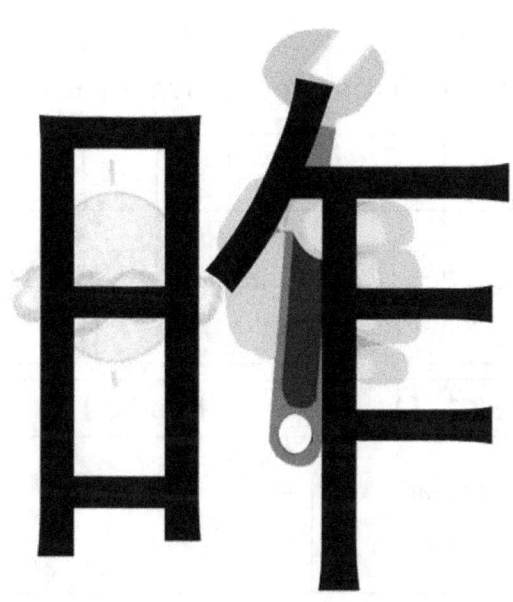

昔 ONCE UPON A TIME

"Once upon a time (昔) there were days (日) with floods (艹) that killed a lot of people"

| 一 | 十 | 艹 | 芷 | 芐 | 昔 | 昔 | | | | | | |

SIMILAR KANJI	Kun (むかし)
借 = Borrow 惜 = Pity	むかし 昔 = Old days, former

昨 YESTERDAY, PREVIOUS

"Create (乍) the best day (日) today out of what you learned yesterday (昨)"

| 丨 | 冂 | 月 | 日 | 日′ | 旷 | 昨 | 昨 | | | | | |

SIMILAR KANJI	ON (サク)	Kun (き)	ODD (ゆう、と)
作 = Make 酢 = Vinegar	さく 昨 = Last (year)	きのう 昨日 = Yesterday	ゆうべ 昨夜 = Last night おととし 一昨年 = Year before last

期 PERIOD, TIME

"At every moon (月) cycle, it is time (期) to fill-up our baskets (其) with crops"

| 一 | 十 | 艹 | 甘 | 甘 | 其 | 其 | 其 | 期 | 期 | 期 | | |

SIMILAR KANJI	ON (キ)		
明 = Bright 朝 = Morning	じき 時期 = Time, season きかん 期間 = Period, term	がっき 学期 = Term (school) きたい 期待 = Expectation	よき 予期 = Expectation ていき 定期 = Fixed term

囲 SURROUND, ENCLOSURE

"The well (井) is inside an enclosure (囲)"

SIMILAR KANJI	ON (イ)		Kun (かこ)
井 = Well 図 = Map	ふんいき 雰囲気 = Atmosphere はんい 範囲 = Extent, scope	しゅうい 周囲 = Surroundings	かこ 囲む = To surround

* The original kanji was 圍 which instead of a well, it was footsteps around the enclosure.

底 BOTTOM, SOLE

"A person bowing (氐) at the bottom (底) of a tent (广)"

SIMILAR KANJI	ON (テイ)	Kun (そこ)
低 = Lower 抵 = Resist	てってい 徹底 = Thoroughness	そこ 底 = Bottom, sole

紀 CHRONICLE, HISTORY

"While working with yarns (糸) the person straightens up (己) and starts telling us a chronicle (紀)"

SIMILAR KANJI	ON (キ)
記 = Scribe 妃 = Queen	せいき 世紀 = Century, era

CHAPTER 12: SPEECH

未	様	極	課	議	詩
245	246	247	248	249	250
調	訓	談	各	願	章
251	252	253	254	255	256
例	他	典	無	然	録
257	258	259	260	261	262
案	法	約			
263	264	265			

未 NOT YET, STILL

"The tree (木) is still growing and not yet (未) ready to bear fruit"

一 二 十 才 未

SIMILAR KANJI	ON (ミ)	Kun (ま)
木 = Tree 末 = End	みらい 未来 = Future	ま 未だ = Yet, still

様 WAY, POLITE SUFFIX

"A good way (様) to have cooperation between tree (木) growers and sheep (羊) farmers is by sharing water (水) resources"

一 十 才 木 木 木 术 栏 样 样 样 様 様

SIMILAR KANJI	ON (ヨウ)		Kun (さま)
羊 = Sheep	よう 様 = Way, manner どうよう 同様 = Identical	ようす 様子 = State of affairs もよう 模様 = Pattern	おうさま 王様 = King さまざま 様々 = Varied

極 VERY, POLES, SETTLEMENT

"The opening (口) between your hand (又) and the tree (木) is very (極) confined and I don't fit in there"

一 十 才 木 木 朽 朽 桓 極 極 極

SIMILAR KANJI	ON (ゴク、キョク)	
術 = Art	ごく 極 = Quite, very	せっきょくてき 積極的 = Positive, active

*This kanji history came from cornering someone against a wall to the extreme.

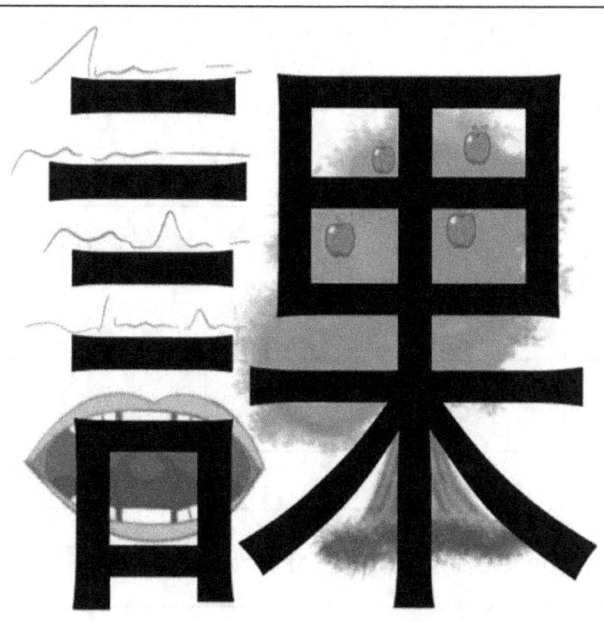

課 CHAPTER, SECTION

"Every chapter (課) in life teaches you words (言) that yield positive results and bear fruits (果)"

SIMILAR KANJI
果 = Fruit
裸 = Naked

ON (カ)

か
課 = Counter for chapters (of a book)

かちょう
課長 = Section manager

議 DELIVERATION, DEBATE

"A good debate (議) must include words (言) of justice (義)"

SIMILAR KANJI
義 = Justice
儀 = Ceremony

ON (ギ)

ぎちょう
議長 = Chairman

ぎいん
議員 = Member of the diet

ぎろん
議論 = Argument

ぎかい
議会 = Diet, congress

ふしぎ
不思議 = Mysterious, wonderful

* The kanji justice (義) comes from a hand holding a tool and a ram, used for sacrifices to God.

詩 POETRY

"The words (言) spoken by everyone that works in the temple (寺) sound like poetry (詩)"

SIMILAR KANJI
侍 = Samurai
待 = Wait

ON (シ)

し
詩 = Poem

しじん
詩人 = Poet

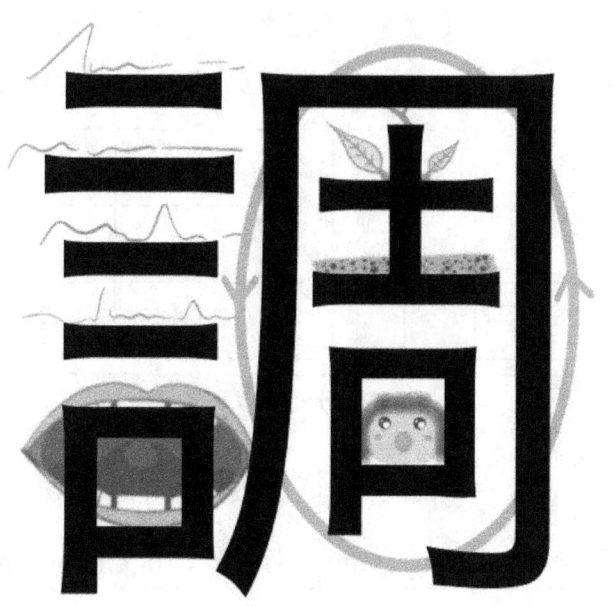

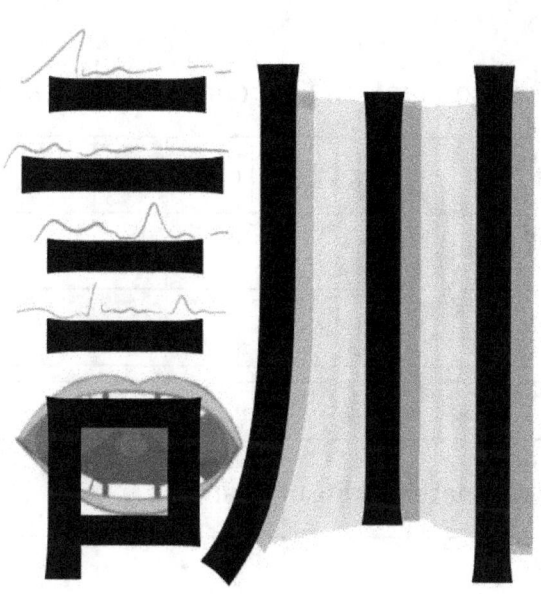

調 TUNE, HARMONIZE, PREPARE

"Please play good tunes (調) with soft words (言) around this circumference (周)"

SIMILAR KANJI	ON (チョウ)		Kun (しら)
週 = Week	じゅんちょう 順調 = Favorable	きょうちょう 強調 = Emphasis	しら 調べる = To investigate
周 = Circumference	ちょうさ 調査 = Investigation	ちょうし 調子 = Tune, tone, key	

訓 INSTRUCTION, EXPLANATION

"Someone who gives a good explanation (訓) can make words (言) flow like a river (川)"

SIMILAR KANJI	ON (クン)	
順 = Order	くん 訓 = Japanese reading of a kanji	くんれん 訓練 = Practice, training
言 = Say, word		

談 DISCUSS, TALK

"Using bad words (言) during a discussion (談) can lead to a blaze (炎) of feelings"

SIMILAR KANJI	ON (ダン)	
淡 = Thin	じょうだん 冗談 = Joke	そうだん 相談 = Consultation
炎 = Blaze		

各 EACH, EVERY

"Every (各) time I go to the temple; I have to clean my feet (夂) at the entrance"

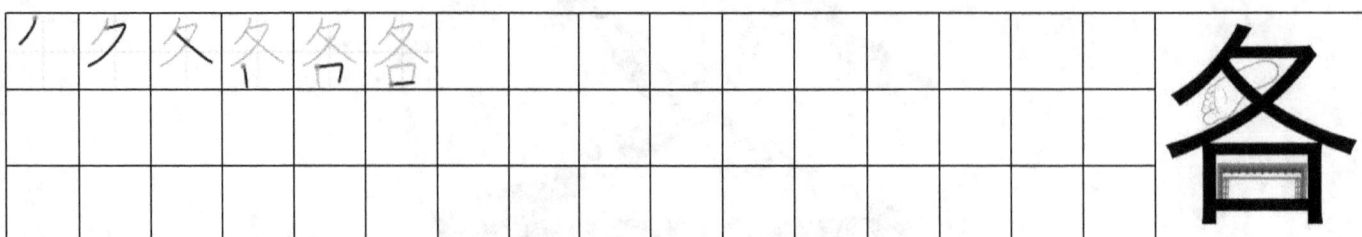

SIMILAR KANJI	ON (カク)	
客 = Guest 名 = Name	かくじ 各自 = Individual	かくち 各地 = Every place

願 PETITION, REQUEST, HOPE

"All the petitions (願) I have in my head (頁) are said out loud in the open field (原)"

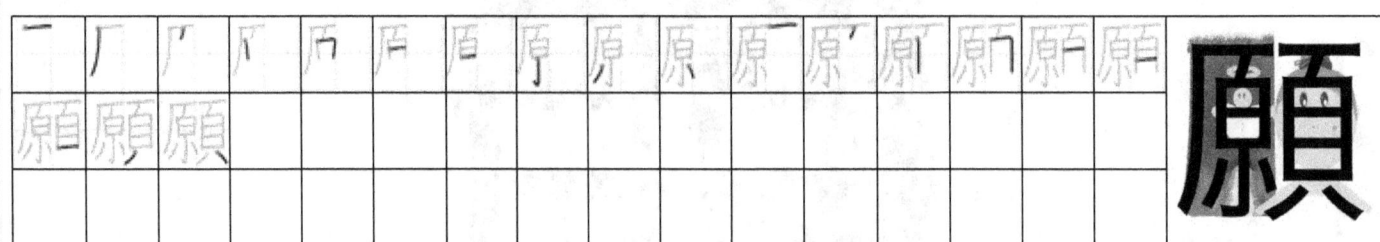

SIMILAR KANJI	Kun (ねが)	
原 = Field 頭 = Head	ねが 願い = Desire, wish	ねが 願う = To desire, to wish

章 BADGE, CHAPTER, COMPOSITION

"When writing a composition (章) I do it early (早) in the morning and I stand up (立) often for ideas"

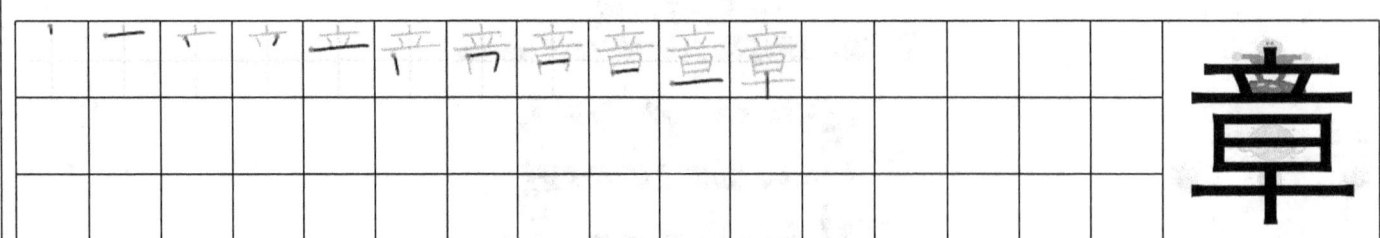

SIMILAR KANJI	ON (ショウ)	
童 = Juvenile 音 = Sound	ぶんしょう 文章 = Sentence	しょう 章 = Chapter, medal

* In the original kanji, what now looks like the radical for "sun", it was the ink used for tattooing, and what looks like "stand up" was a tattooing needle.

例 EXAMPLE

"The person (イ) who properly waits in line (列) sets a good example (例)"

SIMILAR KANJI	ON (レイ)	Kun (たと)
列 = File, row 烈 = Ardent, violent	れい 例 = Example, case	たと 例えば = For example

他 OTHERS, ANOTHER

"That other (他) person (イ) prefers to be (也) near the water"

SIMILAR KANJI	ON (タ)	
池 = Pond 地 = Ground	たにん 他人 = Another person	た その他 = The others

典 CODE, CEREMONY, LAW

"The law (典) books (冊) are on the table (丌)"

SIMILAR KANJI	ON (テン)	
曲 = Bend, music	てんけい 典型 = Type, pattern	じてん 辞典 = Dictionary

* Current form resembles the unrelated 曲 instead of the original 冊

無 NOTHINGNESS, NONE, NOT

"Do not (無) dance (舞) near the fire (灬)"

SIMILAR KANJI	ON (ブ、ム)		Kun (な)
舞 = Dance 焦 = Impatient	む 無 = Nothing ぶじ 無事 = Safety	むだ 無駄 = Futility, waste むし 無視 = Ignore	な 無し = Without な 無くす = To lose (something)

然 SORT OF THING, IF SO

"Cooking meat (月) on fire (灬)? If so (然), don't let your dog (犬) get too close as it is dangerous"

SIMILAR KANJI	ON (ネン、ゼン)		
燃 = Burn 黙 = Silence	てんねん 天然 = Spontaneity ぜんぜん 全然 = (Not) at all	しぜん 自然 = Nature とつぜん 突然 = Abruptly	ぐうぜん 偶然 = (By) chance

録 RECORD

"Take records (録) of the inscriptions found on the already oxidized green (彔) metals (金)"

SIMILAR KANJI	ON (ロク)
緑 = Green 線 = Line	きろく 記録 = Record

案 PLAN, EXPECTATION

"The woman (女) under the roof (宀) writes her expectations (案) on wood (木)"

SIMILAR KANJI
安 = Cheap
委 = Committee

ON (アン)
ていあん 提案 = Proposal	とうあん 答案 = Examination paper
あんない 案内 = Information, guidance	あん 案 = Plan

法 METHOD, LAW, RULE

"In the past (去) those who didn't obey the law (法) didn't get water (氵)"

SIMILAR KANJI
去 = Past
却 = Instead

ON (ホウ)
ほう 法 = Act (law)	けんぽう 憲法 = Constitution
ほうほう 方法 = Method, manner	ぶんぽう 文法 = Grammar

*The original kanji (灋) had a mythical creature that could distinguish right from wrong.

約 PROMISE, APPROXIMATELY

"Let's bind our promises (約) by tying a thread (糸) around a spoon (勺)"

SIMILAR KANJI
的 = Mark, target
酌 = Bar-tending

ON (ヤク)
けいやく 契約 = Contract	こんやく 婚約 = Engagement	よやく 予約 = Reservation
せつやく 節約 = Economizing	やく 約 = Approximately	

CHAPTER 13: NUMBERS & MATH

号	第	番	数	算	点
266	267	268	269	270	271
両	倍	径	兆	億	積
272	273	274	275	276	277

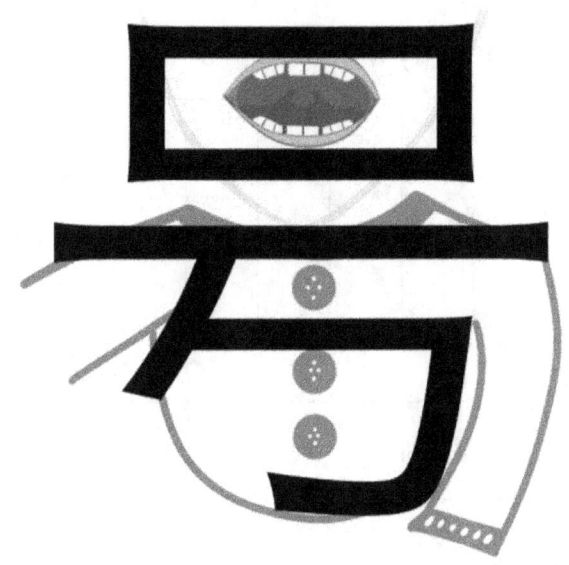

号 NUMBER, ITEM, TITLE

"I breathe (丂) deep and open my mouth (口) a number (号) of times to destress"

SIMILAR KANJI	ON (ゴウ)	
与 = Bestow 汚 = Dirty	ばんごう 番号 = Number	しんごう 信号 = Traffic lights, signal

* The original kanji had a tiger and it meant to shout loudly like a tiger roaring.

第 No., RESIDENCE

"My younger brother (弟) wrote on bamboo (⺮) straps that he was no. (第) one to shoot arrows"

SIMILAR KANJI	ON (ダイ)
弟 = Younger brother 等 = Etc.	しだい 次第 = Order, circumstances, immediately

番 TURN, NUMBER IN A SERIES

"The animal took a number (番) of steps with his paws by the rice field (田)"

SIMILAR KANJI	ON (バン)		
審 = Hearing, trial 藩 = Clan	こうばん 交番 = Police box ばんごう 番号 = Number	じゅんばん 順番 = Order of things いちばん 一番 = Best, number one	ばんぐみ 番組 = Program (TV)

数 NUMBER, FIGURES

"The woman (女) uses a whip (攵) to pull out grains (米) in large numbers (数)"

SIMILAR KANJI	ON (スウ)		Kun (かず、かぞ)
類 = Sort, kind	すう 数 = Several, a number of すうじ 数字 = Numeral, figure	すうがく 数学 = Mathematic	かず 数 = Number, amount かぞ 数える = To count

算 CALCULATE, NUMBER, PROBABILITY

"Using my hands (廾), my eyes (目), and bamboo (⺮) sticks, I count numbers (算)"

SIMILAR KANJI	ON (サン)
昇 = Rise up	よさん 予算 = Estimate, budget

点 SPOT, MARK

"The girl does fortune-telling (占) by reading marks (点) made with fire (灬)"

SIMILAR KANJI	ON (テン)	
店 = Store 占 = Fortune-telling	てん 点 = Spot, dot こうさてん 交差点 = Intersection	けってん 欠点 = Faults ようてん 要点 = Main point

*The original meaning of this kanji was "black spots".

両

倍

径

両 BOTH

"Both (両) sides of the scale must be symmetrical for balance"

一 丁 冂 冋 両 両

SIMILAR KANJI	ON (リョウ)	
丙 = Third class 画 = Brush-stroke	りょうしん 両 親 = Both parents りょうほう 両 方 = Both sides	りょうがえ 両 替 = Money exchange

倍 DOUBLE, TIMES

"That person (亻) splits (咅) the plants twice (倍) for better growth"

丿 亻 亻 仁 仁 位 倍 倍

SIMILAR KANJI	ON (バイ)
剖 = Divide 培 = Cultivate	ばい 倍 = Twice

*The element 咅 was originally a seed that was about to split.

径 DIAMETER, PATH

"I will measure the diameter (径) of the road (亻) by hand (又) to know how much soil (土) we need to fix it"

丿 彳 彳 彳 彳 径 径 径

SIMILAR KANJI	ON (ケイ)	
怪 = Suspicious 経 = Longitude	ちょっけい 直 径 = Diameter	はんけい 半 径 = Radius

兆 TRILLION, OMEN

"The cracks in a tortoise shell were used for omen, and that was the main meaning of the kanji. It was later borrowed to mean trillion (兆)"

SIMILAR KANJI	ON (チョウ)
跳 = Hop 挑 = Challenge	ちょう 兆 = Trillion

億 HUNDRED MILLION

"The number one hundred million (億) is so big that it is hard for the mind (意) of a person (亻) to picture it"

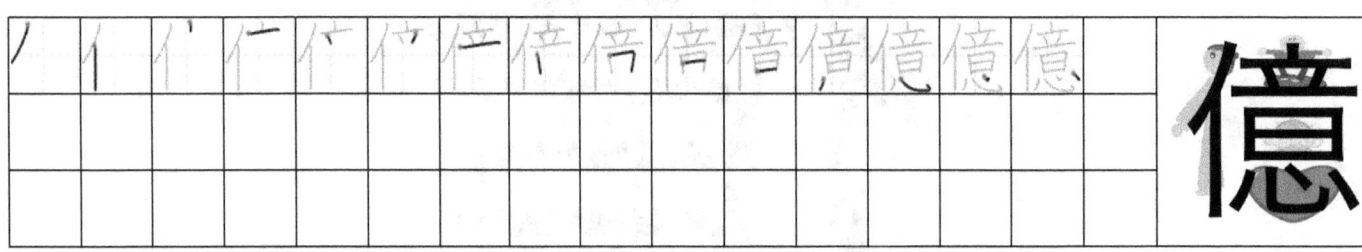

SIMILAR KANJI	ON (オク)
憶 = Recollection 意 = Idea	おく 億 = Hundred million

積 VOLUME, PRODUCT

"We shall increase the volume (積) of grain (禾) and plants (龶) we sell so that our money (貝) also increases"

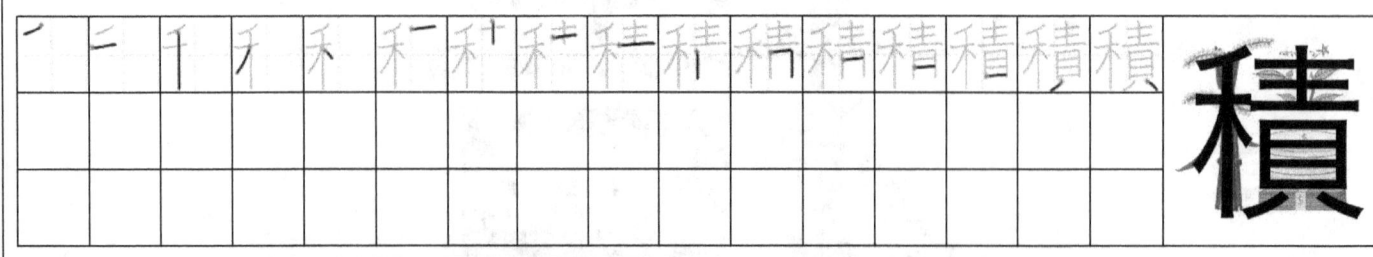

SIMILAR KANJI	ON (セキ)	Kun (つ)
責 = Blame 漬 = Soak	せっきょくてき 積 極 的 = Positive, active	つ 積もる = To pile up

CHAPTER 14: VERBS PART I

決	落	消	浴	泳	漁
278	279	280	281	282	283
泣	活	拾	当	争	挙
284	284	286	287	288	289
折	打	投	固	登	喜
290	291	292	293	294	295
航	商	停	化	伝	付
296	297	298	299	300	301
整	散	救	放	改	包
302	303	304	305	306	307
遊	追	選	連	返	達
308	309	310	311	312	313
辞	曲	覚	労	加	助
314	315	316	317	318	319

決 DECIDE, AGREE UPON

"We decided (決) to break (夬) the water (氵) flow to prevent flooding"

SIMILAR KANJI	ON (ケツ)		Kun (き)
快 = Cheerful 央 = Center	けっしん 決心 = Determination かいけつ 解決 = Settlement	けってい 決定 = Decision	き 決まり = Settlement き 決まる = To be decided

落 FALL, DROP

"Every (各) plant (艹) must get water (氵) so that the leaves don't start falling (落)"

SIMILAR KANJI	Kun (お)
絡 = Coil around	お 落ちる = To fall down

消 EXTINGUISH, TURN OFF

"The meat (月) is burning. Use some water (氵) to extinguish (消) the fire."

SIMILAR KANJI	ON (ショウ)		Kun (き、け)	
宵 = Early night 肖 = Resemblance	しょうぼう 消防 = Fire fighting しょうひ 消費 = Consumption		け 消す = To erase け 消しゴム = Eraser	き 消える = To disappear

浴 BATHE, BE FAVORED WITH

"Let's bathe (浴) in the waters (氵) that surround the valley (谷)"

SIMILAR KANJI	Kun (あ)
谷 = Valley 沿 = Run alongside	あ 浴びる = To bathe in

泳 SWIM

"Sometimes I wish to stay in the water (氵) swimming (泳) for eternity (永)"

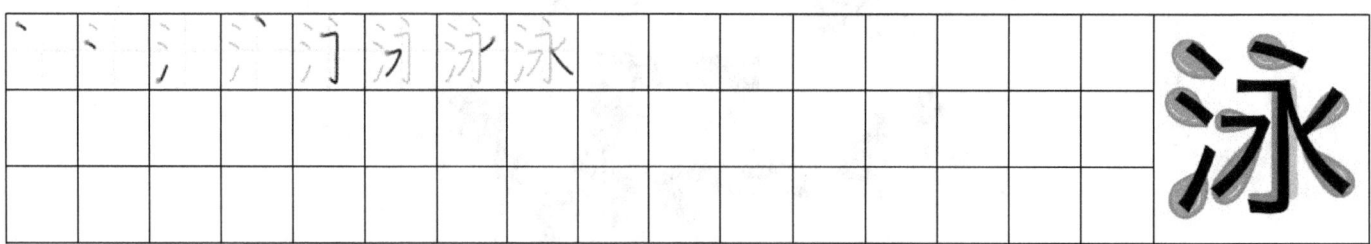

SIMILAR KANJI	ON (エイ)	Kun (およ)
水 = Water 永 = Eternity	すいえい 水泳 = Swimming	およ 泳ぎ = Swimming およ 泳ぐ = To swim

漁 FISHING, FISHERY

"Time to go fishing (漁) with some fish (魚) swimming in the water (氵)"

SIMILAR KANJI	ON (リョウ)
魚 = Fish	りょうし 漁師 = Fisherman

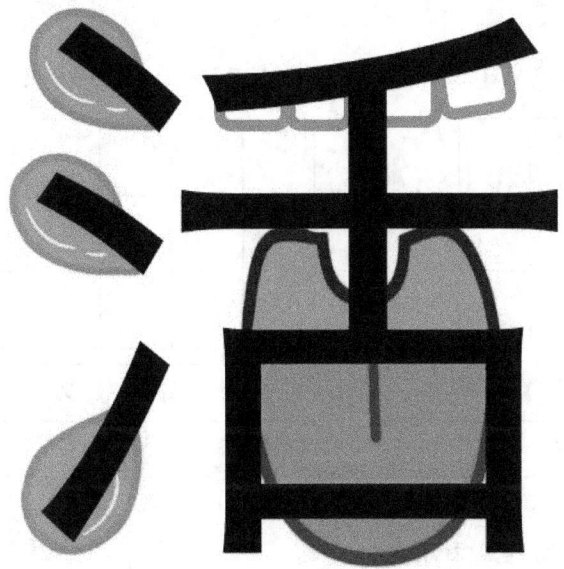

泣 CRY, WEEP

"The man is crying (泣) while standing (立) near sea water (氵)"

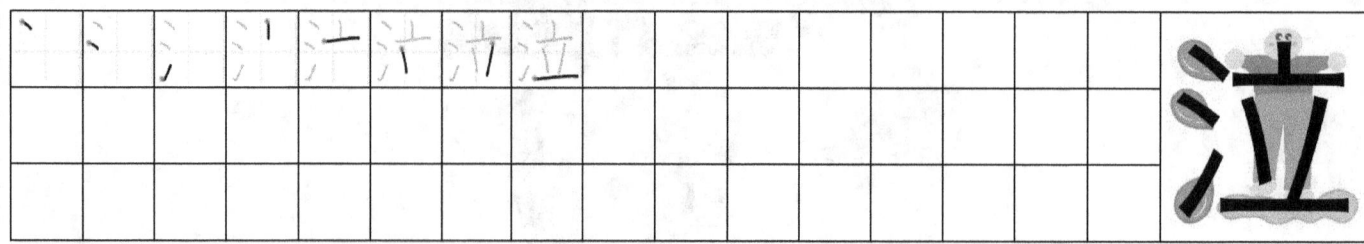

SIMILAR KANJI	Kun (な)
位 = Rank 立 = Stand up	な 泣く = To cry, to weep

活 LIVELY, RESUSCITATION, LIVING

"Part of living (活) is drinking water (氵) and having a refreshing feeling on your tongue (舌)"

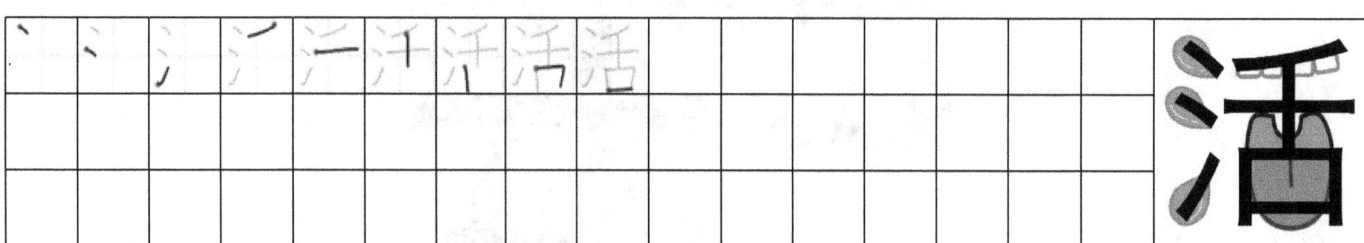

SIMILAR KANJI	ON (カツ)	
括 = Fasten 舌 = Tongue	かっき 活気 = Energy, liveliness かつどう 活動 = Activity	かつよう 活用 = Practical use せいかつ 生活 = Living

拾 PICK UP, GATHER

"I'm picking up (拾) some grains by hand (扌) and making sure the amount fits (合) well in this container"

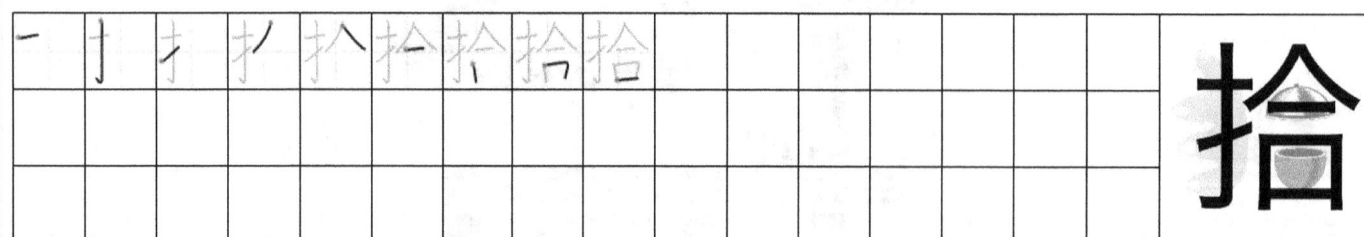

SIMILAR KANJI	Kun (ひろ)
給 = Salary 合 = Fit	ひろ 拾う = To pick up, to gather

当

争

拳

当 HIT, APPROPRIATE

"That small (小) hand (ヨ) can actually hit (当) very hard"

SIMILAR KANJI	ON (トウ)	Kun (あ)
尚 = Furthermore	お弁当 (べんとう) = Boxed lunch 適当 (てきとう) = Suitable	当たる (あ) = To be hit, to be successful

* The original form was 當, but it was later simplified to the current form.

争 CONTEND, DISPUTE

"It is important to dispute (争) everyone's ideas when you govern (尹) a country"

SIMILAR KANJI	ON (ソウ)	
急 = Hurry 事 = Matter	論争 (ろんそう) = Controversy, dispute 戦争 (せんそう) = War	競争 (きょうそう) = Competition

挙 RAISE, PLAN, PROJECT

"Let's raise (挙) all of our hands (手) at the same time!"

SIMILAR KANJI	Kun (あ)
労 = Labor 栄 = Flourish	挙げる (あ) = To raise, to fly

* In the original kanji, the shapes of the multiple hands were clearer than in current form.

折
打
投

折 FOLD, BREAK, FRACTURE

"I fractured (折) my hand (扌) while using the axe (斤)"

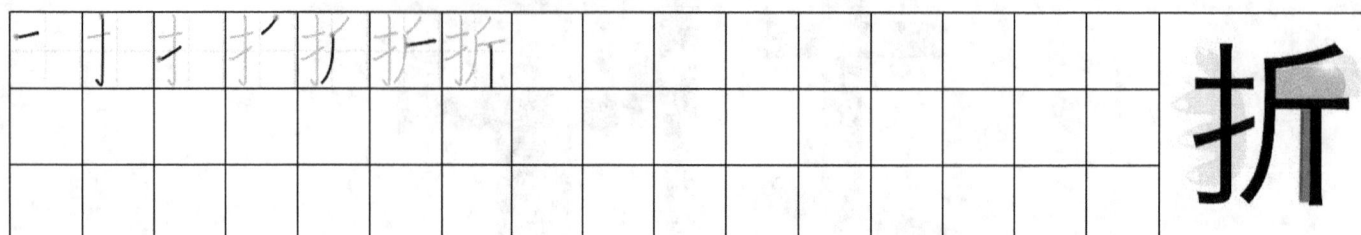

SIMILAR KANJI	ON (セツ)	Kun (お)	
所 = Place 新 = New	こっせつ 骨折 = Bone fracture	お 折る = To break, to fold	お 折れる = To be broken, to be folded

* The original kanji had two plants instead of a hand.

打 STRIKE, HIT

"I hit (打) the street (丁) lamp with my hand (扌) by accident"

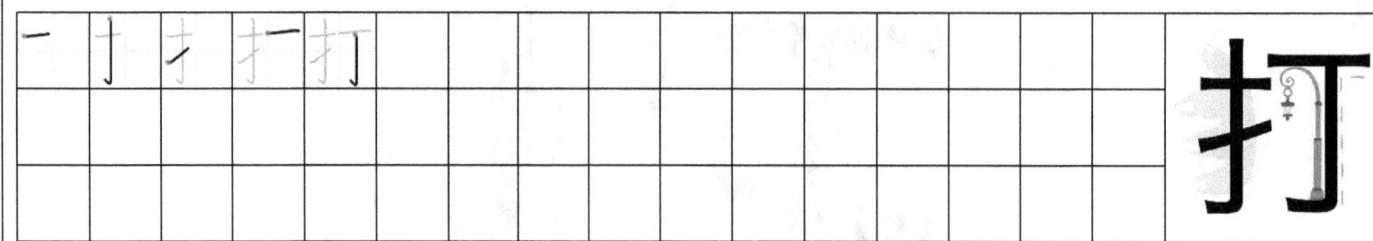

SIMILAR KANJI	Kun (ぶ、う)	
丁 = Street 灯 = Lamp	ぶ 打つ = To hit (a person)	う 打つ = To hit

投 THROW, ABANDON

"I'll be throwing (投) this tool (殳) I'm holding in my hand (扌)"

SIMILAR KANJI	ON (トウ)	Kun (な)
役 = Duty 段 = Steps	とうひょう 投票 = Voting, poll	な 投げる = To throw, to cast

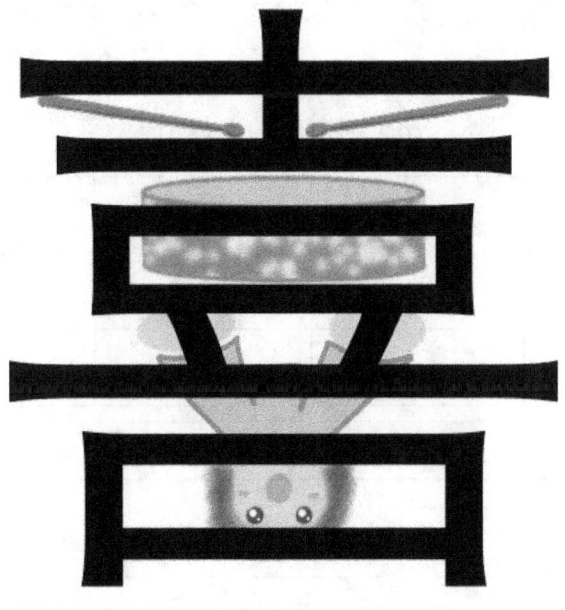

固 HARDEN, CURDLE

"Inside this enclosure (口) there are old (古) graves where the soil has hardened (固)"

SIMILAR KANJI	Kun (かた)	
個 = Individual, Counter for articles 古 = Old	かた 固める = To harden	かた 固い = Hard, solid

登 ASCEND, CLIMB UP

"Giving solid footsteps (癶), I climb up (登) to the top while taking these beans (豆) as an offering to the gods"

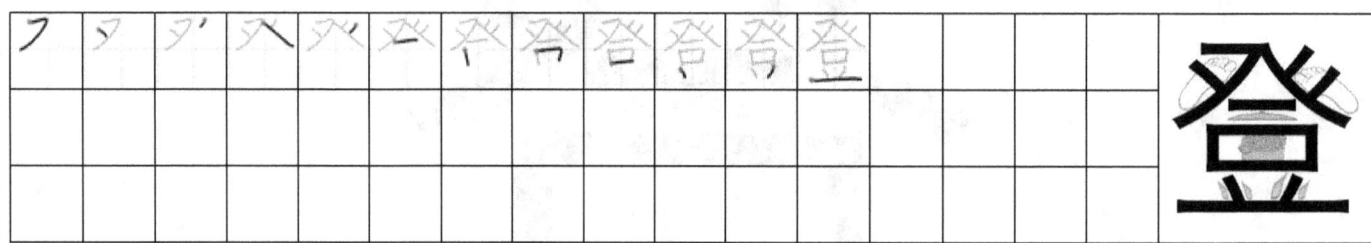

SIMILAR KANJI	ON (ト)	Kun (のぼ)
発 = Departure 澄 = Lucidity	とざん 登山 = Mountain-climbing	のぼ 登る = To climb

喜 REJOICE, TAKE PLEASURE IN

"It's time to rejoice (喜)! Let's play some hand drums (壴) and open our mouths (口) to sing"

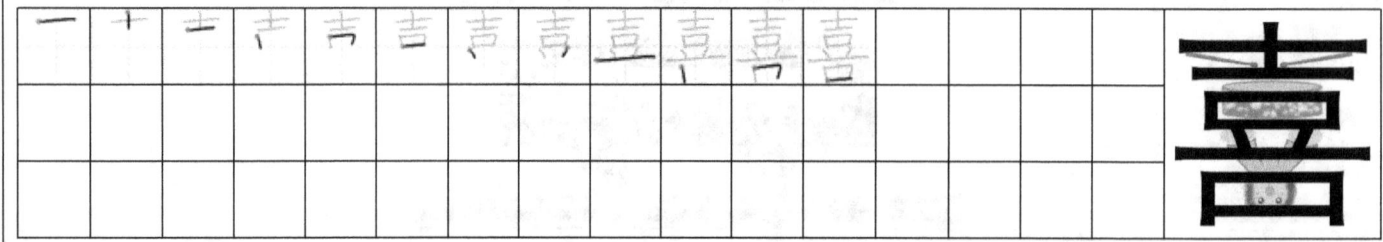

SIMILAR KANJI	Kun (よろこ)	
豆 = Beans 善 = Virtuous	よろこ 喜び = Joy, delight	よろこ 喜ぶ = To be delighted

航 NAVIGATE, SAIL

"Let's navigate (航) by boat (舟) to a high (亢) place"

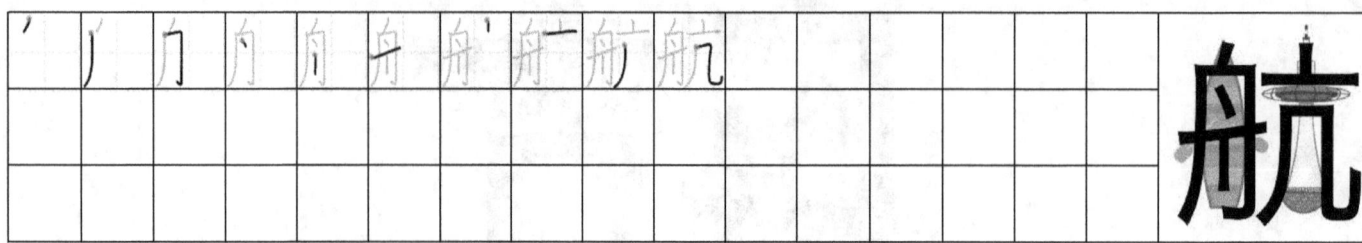

SIMILAR KANJI	ON (コウ)
般 = Carrier 船 = Boat	こうくう 航空 = Aviation, flying

商 MAKE A DEAL, MERCHANT

"The person standing (立) makes a deal (商) for the price of the box (口)"

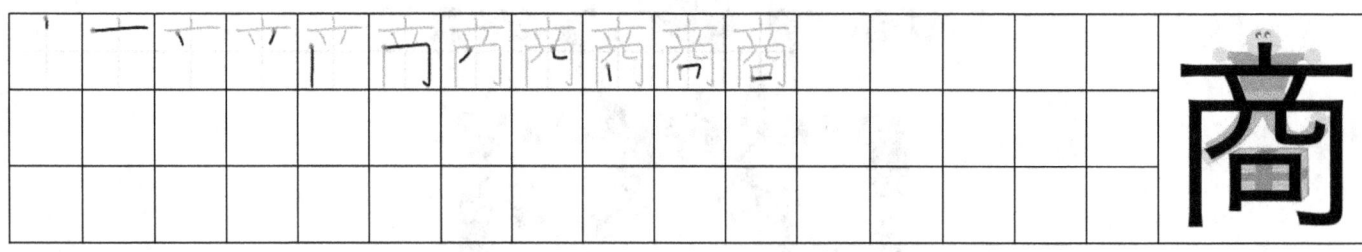

SIMILAR KANJI	ON (ショウ)	
滴 = Drop 高 = Tall	しょうにん 商人 = Trader しょうひん 商品 = Commodity, goods	しょうばい 商売 = Trade, business

停 HALT, STOPPING

"The person (亻) stops (停) at the pavilion (亭) for a convention"

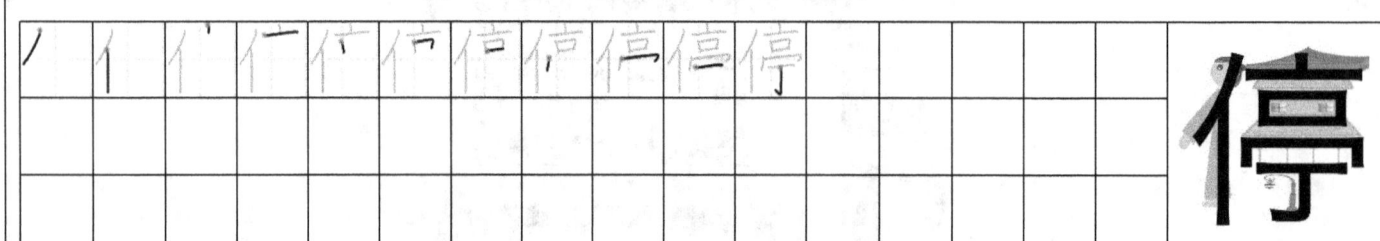

SIMILAR KANJI	ON (テイ)
亭 = Pavilion	ていりゅうじょ 停留所 = Bus or tram stop

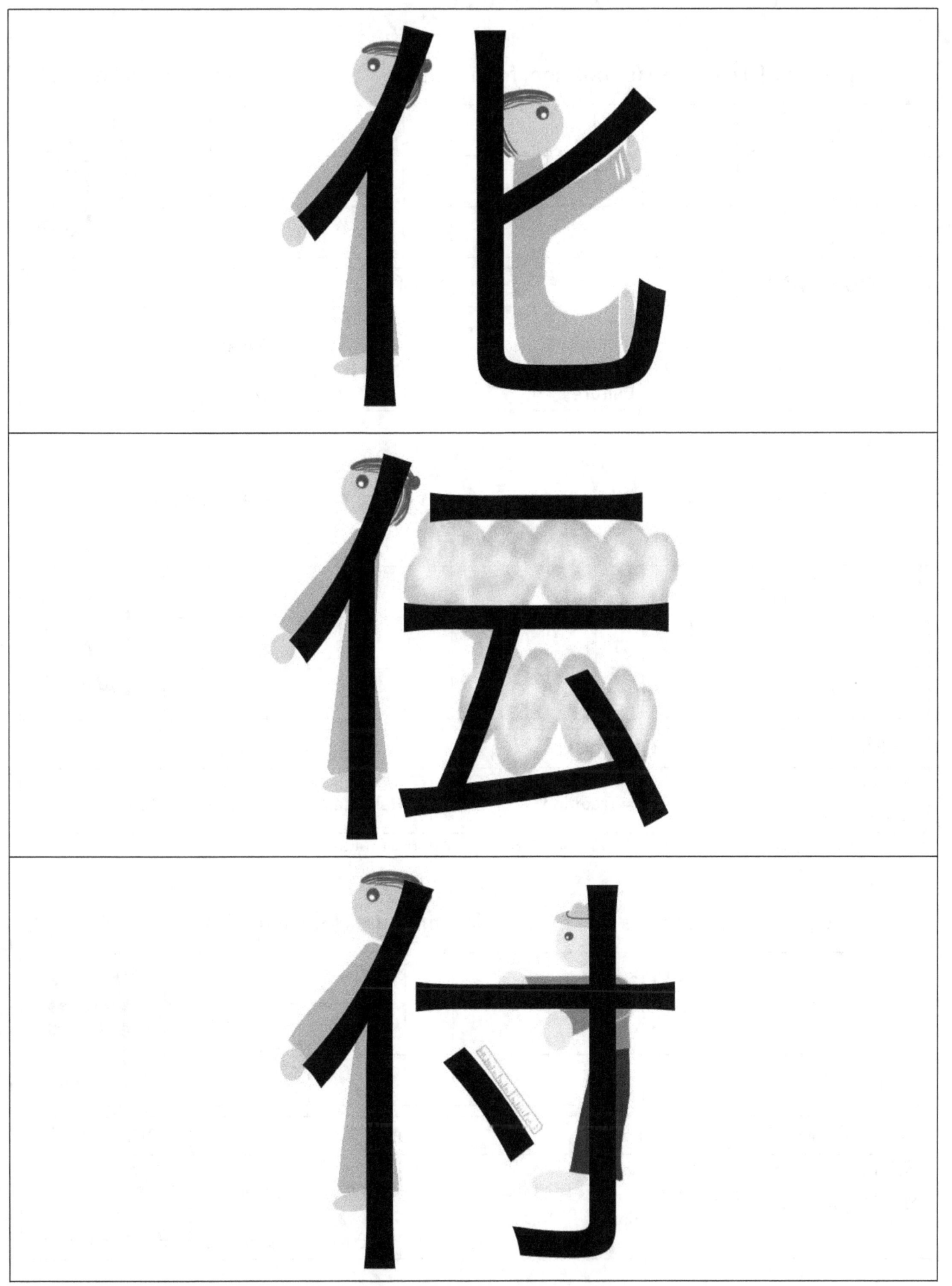

化
伝
待

化 CHANGE, INFLUENCE

"The person (亻) changes (化) position, from standing up to siting down like a ladle (匕)"

ノ 亻 亻́ 化

SIMILAR KANJI	ON (カ、ケ)	
代 = Convert 北 = North	かがく 化学 = Chemistry ぶんか 文化 = Culture	へんか 変化 = Change けしょう 化粧 = Make-up (cosmetic)

伝 TRANSMIT, REPORT

"The person (亻) wonders how to transmit (伝) a message far beyond the clouds (云)"

ノ 亻 亻́ 伝 伝

SIMILAR KANJI	ON (デン)	Kun (つた)
仏 = Buddha 転 = Revolve	でんとう 伝統 = Tradition	てつだ 手伝い = Help, helper	つた 伝える = To report

* The original kanji (傳) was simplified to its current form and it meant a post-chariot that delivered letters.

付 ATTACH, ADHERE

"The person (亻) adheres (付) to any safety measures (寸) and rules in their job"

ノ 亻 亻́ 付 付

SIMILAR KANJI	ON (フ)	Kun (つ)	ODD (つけ)
代 = Convert 寸 = Measurement	きふ 寄付 = Contribution	つ 付ける = To attach きづ 気付く = To notice	お 追い付く = To reach つあ 付き合い = Association	ひづけ 日付 = Date うけつけ 受付 = Receipt

244

整 ORGANIZE, ARRANGING

"The hand hits (攵) the bundle (束) of wood in order to arrange (整) it in the correct (正) sequence"

SIMILAR KANJI	ON (セイ)
正 = Correct 裂 = Split	せいり 整理 = Sorting, arrangement

散 SCATTER, DISPERSE

"The hand hits (攵) the meat (月) to disperse (散) it and adds plant (艹) spices on it"

SIMILAR KANJI	ON (サン)	
借 = Borrow	さんぽ 散歩する = To stroll	さんぽ 散歩 = Stroll

救 SAVE, HELP

"His request (求) is to help (救) those who get hit (攵) without justification"

SIMILAR KANJI	Kun (すく)
求 = Request 球 = Ball	すく 救う = To rescue from

放

改

包

放 SET FREE, EMIT

"The hand hits (攵) everything in all directions (方) trying to set itself free (放)"

SIMILAR KANJI	ON (ホウ)	Kun (はな)
坊 = Boy 妨 = Disturb	ほうそう 放送 = Broadcast	はな 放す = To separate, to set free

改 REFORMATION, MODIFY

"In the old days, reformations (改) were about hitting (攵) people to straighten (己) them up"

SIMILAR KANJI	ON (カイ)
攻 = Aggression 功 = Achievement	かいぜん 改善 = Betterment, improvement

包 WRAP, PACK UP

"The body of a pregnant woman wraps (包) up the baby in a way that will keep him safe"

SIMILAR KANJI	Kun (つつ)	
抱 = Hug 泡 = Bubbles	つつ 包み = Bundle, package つつ 包む = To wrap up	こづつみ 小包 = Parcel, package

遊

追

選

遊 PLAY

"The child (子) plays (遊) with the flag pole (㫃) that's on the road (辶)"

SIMILAR KANJI	Kun (あそ)	
旋 = Rotation	あそ 遊ぶ = To play, to make a visit	あそ 遊び = Playing

追 CHASE, FOLLOW

"The military would chase (追) stacks (㠯) of things found on the road (辶) in order to protect themselves from harm"

SIMILAR KANJI	Kun (お)	
迫 = Urge 泊 = Overnight stay	お　つ 追い付く = To reach	お 追う = To chase

選 ELECT, CHOOSE

"Always choose (選) a road (辶) together (共) with the person you trust the most"

SIMILAR KANJI	ON (セン)	Kun (えら)
巽 = Southeast	せんしゅ 選手 = Player (in game), team せんたく 選択 = Selection, choice	えら 選ぶ = To choose, to select

連 TAKE ALONG, JOIN

"For this road (辶) trip, let's take everyone along (連) in our car (車)"

SIMILAR KANJI	ON (レン)		Kun (つ)
車 = Car 運 = Carry	れんそう 連想 = Suggestion かんれん 関連 = Relation, connection	れんぞく 連続 = Serial, consecutive	つ 連れ = Companion つ 連れる = To bring along

返 RETURN, REPAY

"When we try to return (返) to the past it goes against (反) moving forward on life's road (辶)"

SIMILAR KANJI	ON (ヘン)	Kun (かえ)
坂 = Slope 板 = Plank	へんじ 返事 = Reply	く かえ 繰り返す = To repeat かえ 返す = To return (something)

達 ATTAIN, REACH, PLURAL SUFFIX

"The sheep (羊) reached (達) the plants (土) on the other side of the road (辶)"

SIMILAR KANJI	ON (タツ)		Kun (たち)
運 = Carry 連 = Take along	はったつ 発達 = Growth たっ 達する = To reach	はいたつ 配達 = Delivery じょうたつ 上達 = Improvement	ともだち 友達 = Friend

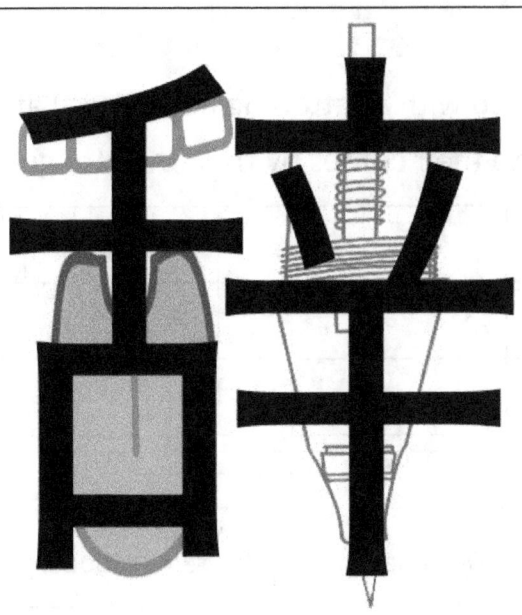

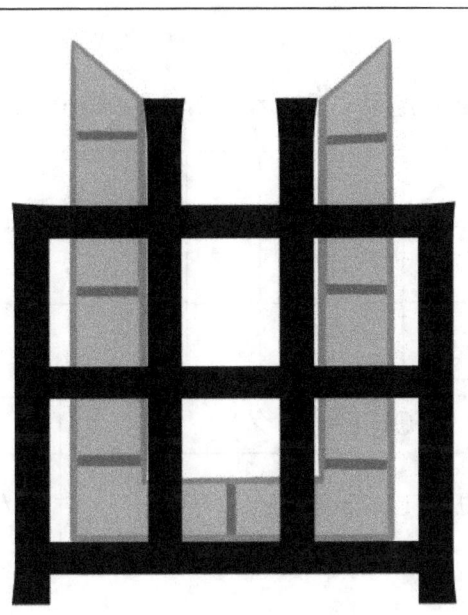

辞 RESIGN, WORD

"Criminals used to be marked with a tattooing needle (辛) after confessing and resigning (辞) to their crimes by their own tongue (舌)"

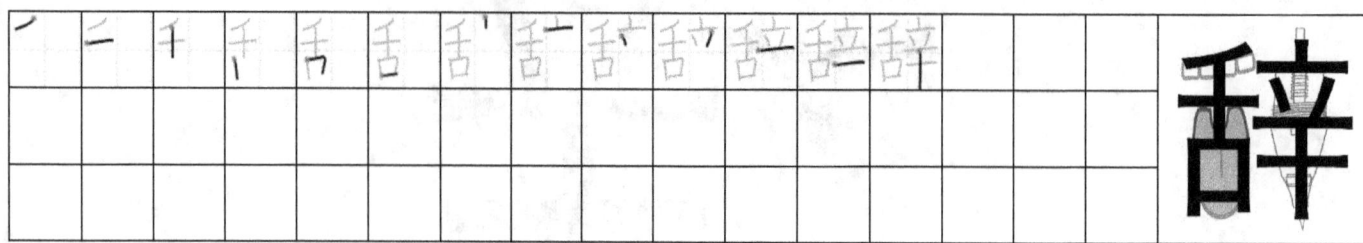

SIMILAR KANJI	ON (ジ)	Kun (や)
辛 = Bitter, spicy 梓 = Catalpa tree	じしょ 辞書 = Dictionary　　じてん 辞典 = Dictionary	や 辞める = To retire

曲 MUSIC, BEND

"Bamboo can be bent (曲) and changed into different shapes"

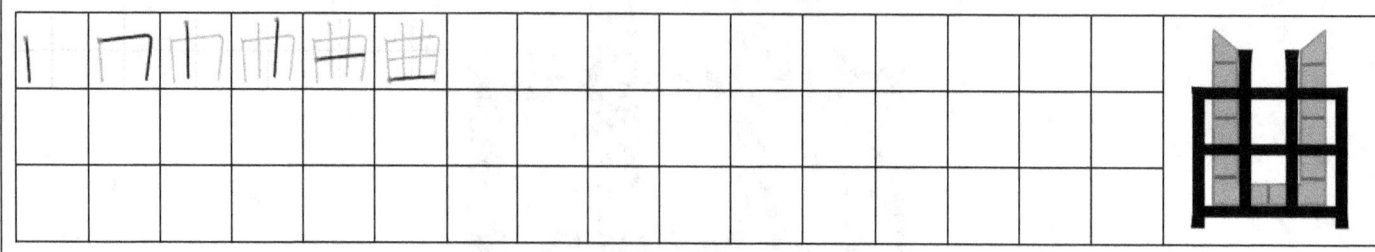

SIMILAR KANJI	ON (キョク)	Kun (ま)
典 = Code 由 = A reason	さっきょく 作曲 = Composition	ま 曲がる = To turn, to bend

覚 MEMORIZE, REMEMBER

"To remember (覚) things better, one has to focus more and look (見) at things closer"

SIMILAR KANJI	ON (カク)	Kun (おぼ、さ)	
賞 = Prize 党 = Party	かくご 覚悟 = Resolution, resignation かんかく 感覚 = Sense	おぼ 覚える = To remember さ 覚める = To wake up	さ 覚ます = to awaken

*The top element in this kanji came originally from 學 which meant to help each other. It is the same as in the kanji for learning 学

労

加

助

労 LABOR, TROUBLE

"Let's light up some fire (火) at night time so we can continue to labor (労) with all our strength (力)"

SIMILAR KANJI	ON (ロウ)	
力 = Strength 栄 = Flourish	ろうどう 労働 = Manual labor	くろう 苦労 = Troubles, hardships

加 ADD, INCREASE

"When shouting, you feel the increase (加) of strength (力) of your mouth (口)"

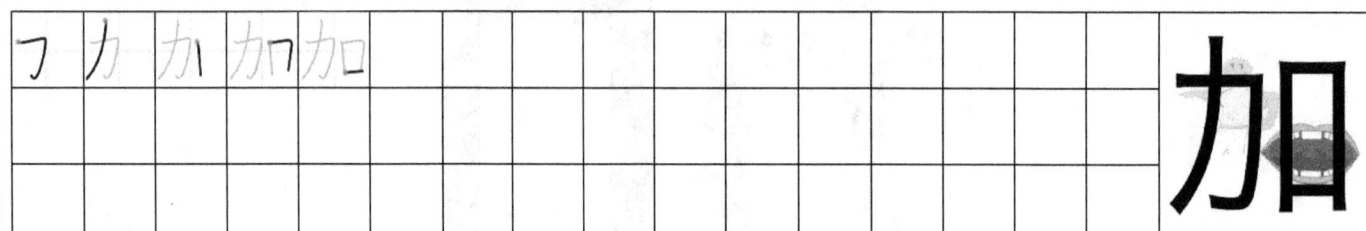

SIMILAR KANJI	ON (カ)		Kun (くわ)
和 = Harmony 如 = Likeness	かげん 加減 = Degree, extent ぞうか 増加 = Increase	さんか 参加 = Participation	くわ 加える = To sum up くわ 加わる = To join in

助 HELP, RESCUE

"Let's pray and ask for help (助) and strength (力) from our ancestors (且)"

SIMILAR KANJI	ON (ジョ)		Kun (たす)
肋 = Rib	えんじょ 援助 = Assistance, aid じょしゅ 助手 = Helper, tutor	きゅうじょ 救助 = Relief, aid	たす 助ける = To help, to save

CHAPTER 15: VERBS PART II

失	求	笑	察	守	定
320	321	322	323	324	325
飛	要	養	息	刷	初
326	327	328	329	330	331
成	配	照	晴	唱	得
332	333	334	335	336	337
委	交	申	鳴	向	告
338	339	340	341	342	343
競	祝	焼	殺	取	受
344	345	346	347	348	349
省	植	置	育	望	勝
350	351	352	353	354	355
負	費	参	練	続	結
356	357	358	359	360	361

失

求

笑

失 LOSE, ERROR

"My husband (夫) was holding something in his hand but then he lost (失) it"

SIMILAR KANJI	ON (シツ)		Kun (うしな)
夫 = Husband 矢 = Arrow	しつぎょう 失業 = Unemployment しつぼう 失望 = Disappointment, despair	しっぱい 失敗 = Failure	うしな 失う = To lose

求 REQUEST, WANT

"A person kneels down to make his request (求)"

SIMILAR KANJI	ON (キュウ)	Kun (もと)
来 = To come 永 = Eternity	せいきゅう 請求 = Claim, demand ようきゅう 要求 = Request, requisition	もと 求める = To seek, to request

*The kanji was originally created to mean fur coat, but eventually changed.

笑 LAUGH

"The young (夭) man is dancing and laughing (笑) underneath the swaying bamboo (⺮)"

SIMILAR KANJI	Kun (わら、え)	
答 = Answer	わら 笑い = Laugh, laughter わら 笑う = To laugh	ほほえ 微笑む = To smile えがお 笑顔 = Smiling face

*The element 夭 originally meant young as seen in this kanji. It eventually changed to "Die young". Do not confuse with 天

察

守

定

察 GUESS, JUDGE

"During the offering ritual (祭) under this roof (宀) no one is allowed to judge (察) others"

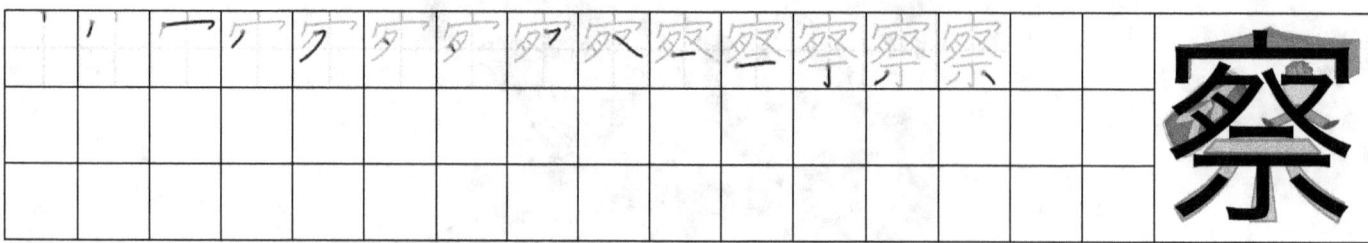

SIMILAR KANJI	ON (サツ)	
祭 = Ritual 擦 = Rub	かんさつ 観察 = Observation しんさつ 診察 = Medical examination	けいさつ 警察 = Police

守 GUARD, PROTECT

"He measures (寸) the roof (宀) to make sure it will be able to securely protect (守) the home"

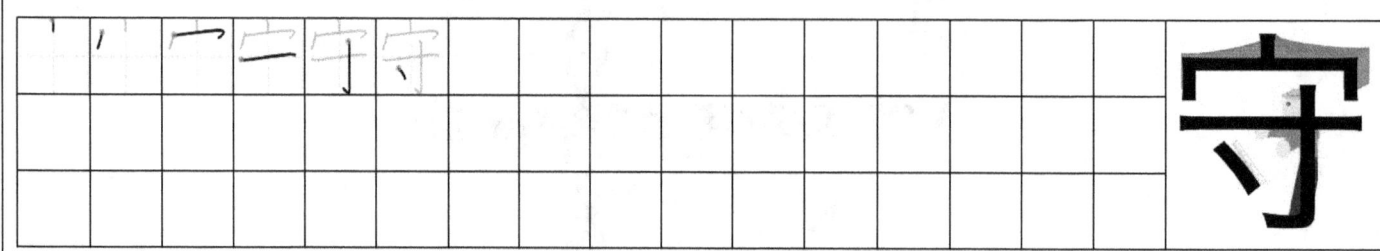

SIMILAR KANJI	ON (ス)	Kun (まも)
字 = Character 寸 = Measurement	るす 留守 = Absense	まも 守る = To protect, to obey

定 DETERMINE, ESTABLISH

"I've established (定) myself under this roof (宀) and settled my feet (足) in there"

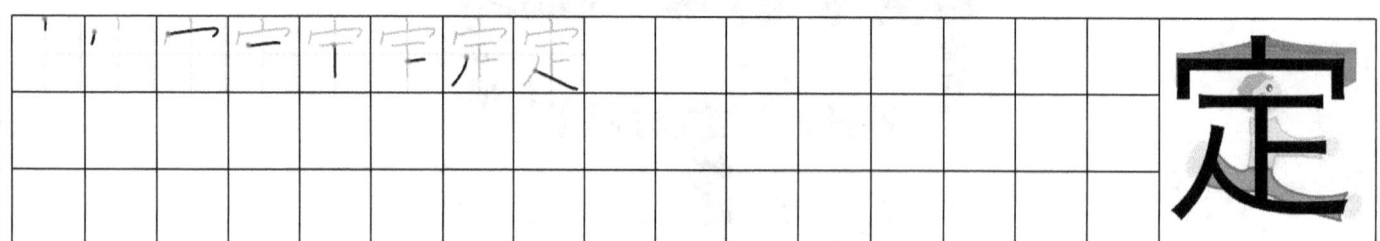

SIMILAR KANJI	ON (テイ、ジョウ)		
足 = Leg	あんてい 安定 = Stability けってい 決定 = Decision	ていき 定期 = Fixed term かんじょう 勘定 = Calculation	ひてい 否定 = Negation よてい 予定 = Arrangement

飛 FLY, SCATTER

"The bird is flying (飛) upwards"

SIMILAR KANJI	ON (ヒ)		Kun (と)	
升 = Measuring box	ひこうき 飛行機 = Airplane ひこうじょう 飛行場 = Airport	ひこう 飛行 = Aviation	と 飛ばす = To skip over と　だ 飛び出す = To jump out	と 飛ぶ = To fly

要 NEED, MAIN POINT

"Women (女) need (要) special coverings (西) in some countries"

SIMILAR KANJI	ON (ヨウ)			Kun (い)
栗 = Chestnut 票 = Ballot	ようそ 要素 = Element じゅよう 需要 = Demand	しゅよう 主要 = Chief, main よう 要するに = After all	ようてん 要点 = Main point ひつよう 必要 = Necessary	い 要る = To be needed

養 FOSTER, BRING UP

"We foster (養) sheep (羊) by getting them to eat (食) properly"

SIMILAR KANJI	ON (ヨウ)
食 = Eat, food	えいよう 栄養 = Nutrition

息

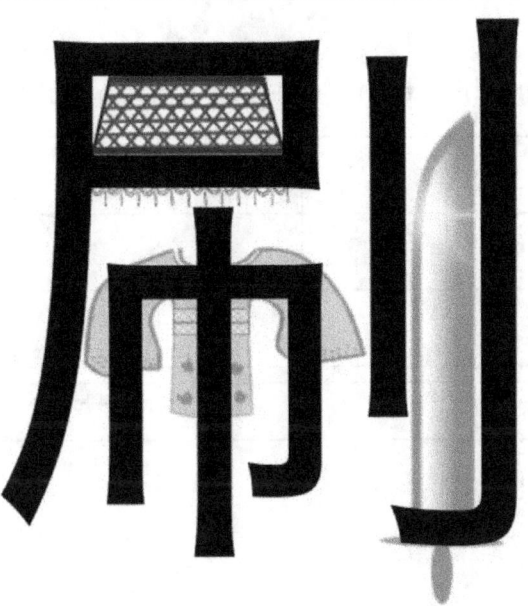

刷

初

息 BREATH

"Take a moment for yourself (自) to breath (息) deep and calm your heart (心)"

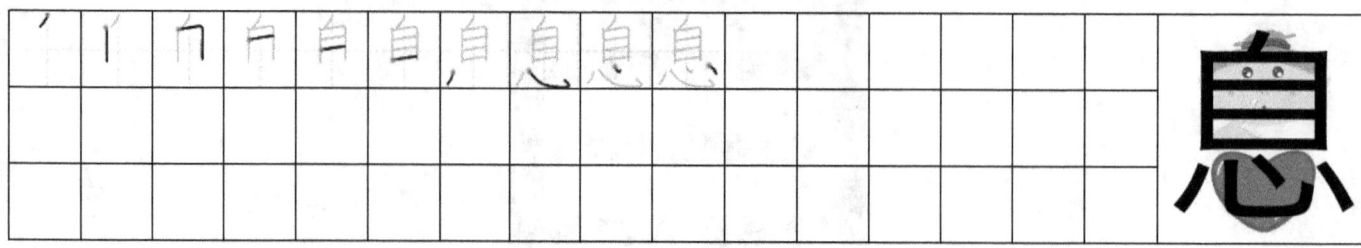

SIMILAR KANJI	Kun (いき)	ODD (む)
自 = Oneself 思 = Think	いき 息 = Breath	むすこ 息子 = Son

刷 PRINT, BRUSH

"Using a knife (刂) as a brush to print (刷) patterns on clothes (巾) and other fabrics"

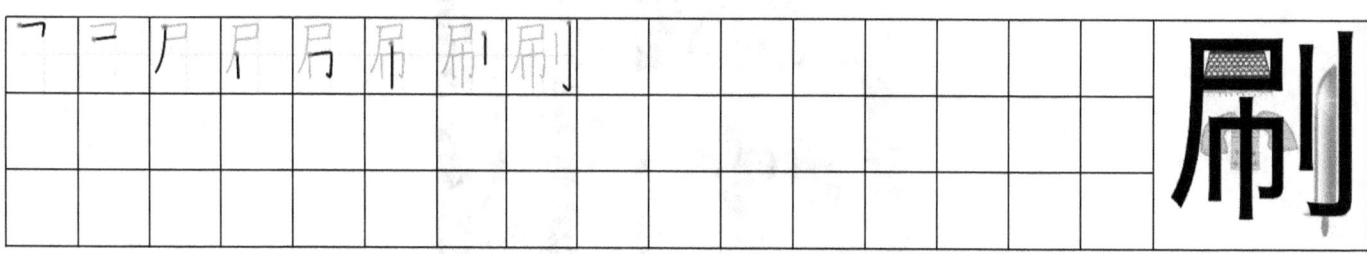

SIMILAR KANJI	ON (サツ)
刺 = Pierce 制 = Law	いんさつ 印刷 = Printing

初 FIRST TIME, BEGINNING, START

"In order to start (初) making clothes (ネ), the first thing is to cut the fabric with a knife (刀)"

SIMILAR KANJI	ON (ショ)	Kun (はじ)
刀 = Sword 切 = Cut	さいしょ 最初 = Beginning	はじ 初めて = For the first time はじ 初め = Beginning

成

配

照

成 TURN INTO, BECOME

"This halberd (戈) is used to pound metals and turn (成) them into different shapes"

SIMILAR KANJI	ON (セイ)			Kun (な)
城 = Castle 盛 = Prosper	かんせい 完成 = Completion せいちょう 成長 = Growth	せいこう 成功 = Success せいせき 成績 = Results	せいじん 成人 = Adult	な 成る = To become

配 DISTRIBUTE, EXCILE

"The person straightens (己) up to distribute (配) the wine vessel (酉)"

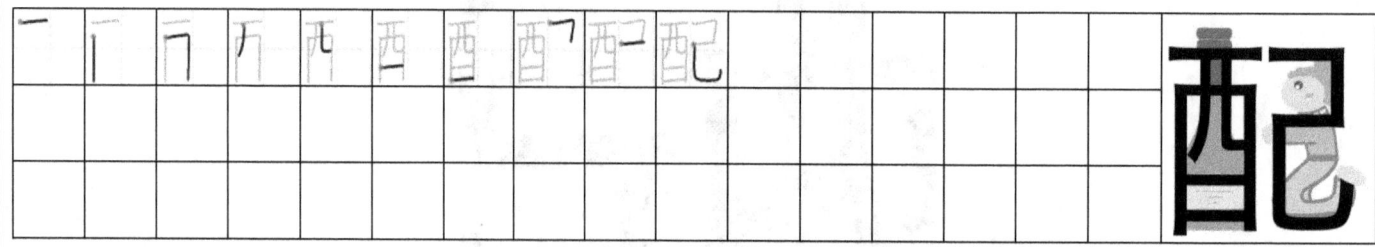

SIMILAR KANJI	ON (ハイ)	
記 = Scribe 妃 = Queen	しはい 支配 = Rule, control しんぱい 心配 = Worry, concern	はいたつ 配達 = Delivery

昭 ILLUMINATE, SHINE

"Both, the bright (昭) sun (日) and fire (灬) shine (照)"

SIMILAR KANJI	Kun (て)	
昭 = Bright	て 照らす = To shine on	て 照る = To shine

晴
唱
得

晴 CLEAR UP

"The blue (青) sky has cleared up (晴) and the sun (日) is out again"

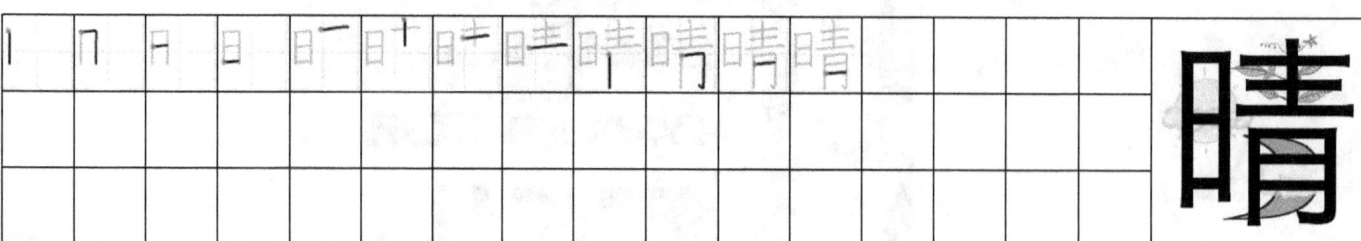

SIMILAR KANJI	Kun (は)	
清 = Pure 青 = Blue	は 晴れ = Clear weather すば 素晴らしい = Wonderful	は 晴れる = To be sunny

唱 CHANT, RECITE

"The mouth (口) recites (唱) a poem about many suns (日)"

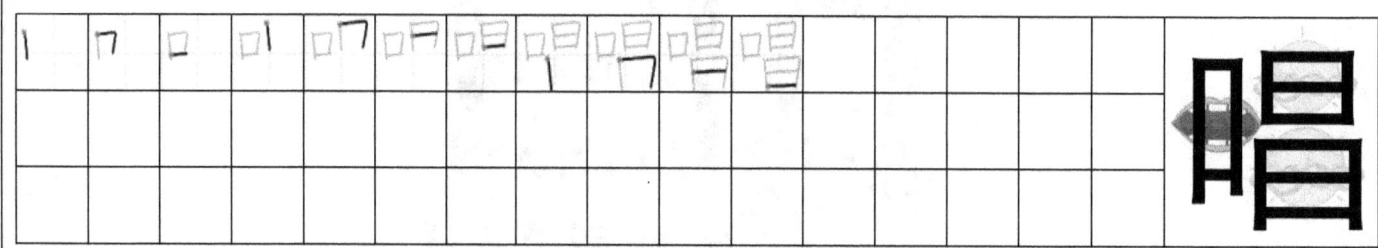

SIMILAR KANJI	Kun (とな)
晶 = Clear 品 = Goods	とな 唱える = To chant, to recite

得 GAIN, EARN, PROFIT

"I go to work on the road (彳) at dawn (旦) and earn (得) my share"

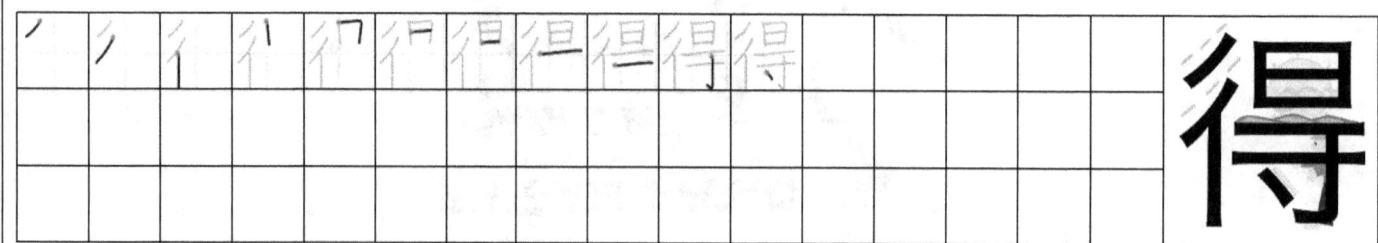

SIMILAR KANJI	ON (トク)	Kun (え、う)
待 = Wait 持 = Hold	なっとく 納得 = Consent, assent とくい 得意 = Pride, triumph	う 得る = To get, to acquire, to be able to え 得る = To get, to earn

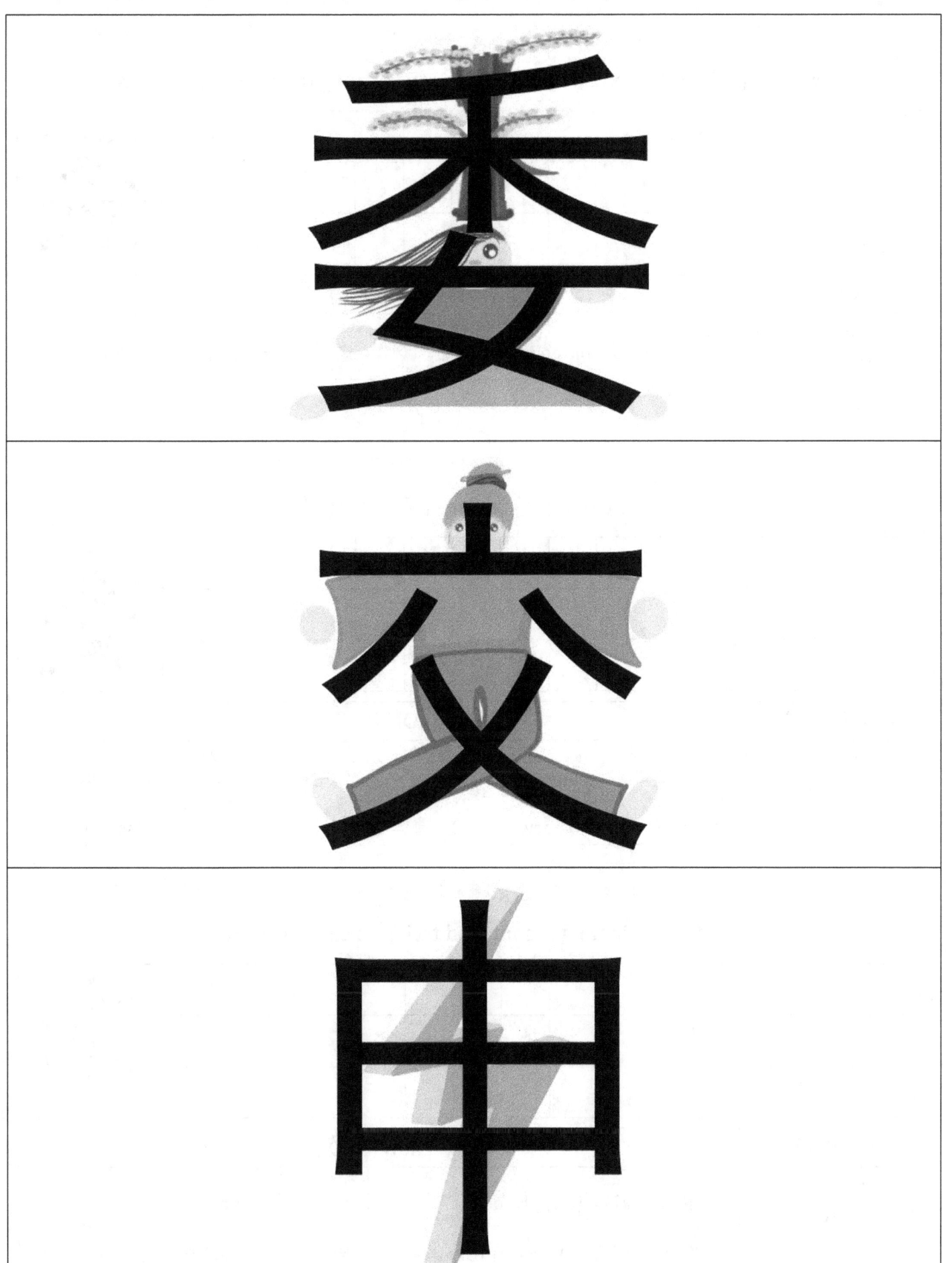

委 COMMITTEE, ENTRUST TO

"Women (女) have been entrusted (委) with carrying the grain (禾) plants"

SIMILAR KANJI	ON (イ)	
季 = Season 柔 = Tender	いいん 委員 = Committee member	いにん 委任 = Entrusting, delegation

交 CROSS, MIXING

"The dad (父) crosses (交) his legs"

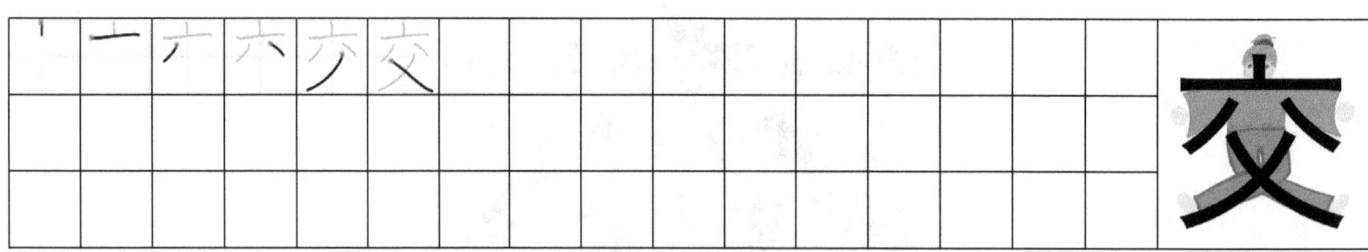

SIMILAR KANJI	ON (コウ)		
父 = Dad 文 = Sentence	こうさてん 交差点 = Intersection がいこう 外交 = Diplomacy	こうかん 交換 = Exchange こうつう 交通 = Traffic	こうばん 交番 = Police box こうさい 交際 = Association

申 HAVE THE HONOR TO, SAY

"In the old days, lighting meant God trying to say (申) something"

SIMILAR KANJI	Kun (もう)	
田 = Rice field 由 = A reason	もう こ 申し込む = To apply for もう あ 申し上げる = (Humble) To say	もう わけ 申し訳 = Apology, excuse もう 申す = (Humble) To say, to be called

鳴 CHIRP, BARK, CRY

"My bird (鳥) chirps (鳴) louder than my mouth (口) can scream!"

| 丶 | 丨 | 口 | 口ˊ | 口ㇵ | 口ㇵ | 口ㇵ | 吖 | 咱 | 鳴 | 鳴 | 鳴 | 鳴 | 鳴 | | | 鳴 |

SIMILAR KANJI	Kun (な)	
鳥 = Bird 島 = Island	な 鳴く = To make sound (of an animal)	な 鳴る = To sound, to ring

向 YONDER, FACING, BEYOND

"The window opening (口) is facing (向) north"

| 丿 | 丨 | 冂 | 向 | 向 | 向 | | | | | | | | | | | 向 |

SIMILAR KANJI	ON (コウ)	Kun (む)		
同 = Same 回 = Round	けいこう 傾 向 = Tendency ほうこう 方 向 = Direction	む 向こう = Over there む 向かう = To face	む 向かい = Facing む 向ける = To point	む 向く = To face (e.g. east)

告 REVELATION, TELL, INFORM

"Please inform (告) the chief that the cow (牛) escaped through the opening (口)"

| 丿 | 一 | 十 | 牛 | 牛 | 告 | 告 | | | | | | | | | | 告 |

SIMILAR KANJI	ON (コク)	
先 = Before 吉 = Good luck	けいこく 警 告 = Warning, advice ほうこく 報 告 = Report, information	こうこく 広 告 = Advertisement

*The original meaning of the kanji was to raise cattle.

競

祝

燒

競 COMPETE WITH, CONTEST, RACE

"The standing (立) crowd see the two brothers (兄) competing (競) with each other"

SIMILAR KANJI	ON (キョウ)	
兄 = Older brother	きょうそう 競争 = Competition	きょうぎ 競技 = Game, match

祝 CELEBRATE, CONGRATULATE

"The elder brother (兄) celebrates (祝) his wedding in front of the altar (ネ)"

SIMILAR KANJI	Kun (いわ)	
況 = Condition 兄 = Older brother	いわ お祝い = Congratulation いわ 祝う = To congratulate, to celebrate	いわ 祝い = Celebration, festival

焼 BAKE, BURNING

"The fire (火) burns (焼) nicely inside the high (尭) temperature kiln"

SIMILAR KANJI	Kun (や)	
尭 = High 暁 = Dawn	や 焼く = To bake, grill	や 焼ける = To burn

殺

取

受

殺 KILL, MURDER

"Use this tool (殳) to kill (殺) the animal that is destroying all the trees (木)"

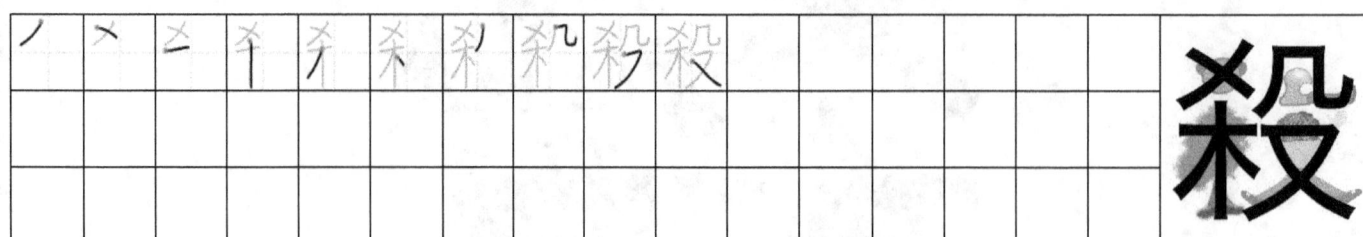

SIMILAR KANJI	ON (サツ)	Kun (ころ)
役 = Duty 投 = Throw	じさつ 自殺 = Suicide	ころ 殺す = To kill

取 TAKE, FETCH

"Warriors used to take (取) their enemy's ear (耳) in their hands (又) when victorious"

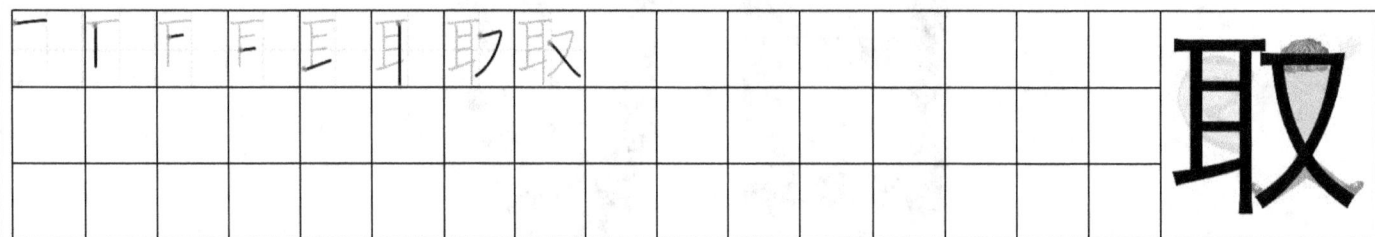

SIMILAR KANJI	Kun (と)		
双 = Pair 収 = Income	と 取る= To take something と あ 取り上げる = To take up	と 取れる= To come off と か 取り換える= To exchange	う と 受け取る= To receive

受 ACCEPT, UNDERGO

"She accepts (受) his proposal while his hand (手) holds her hand (又)"

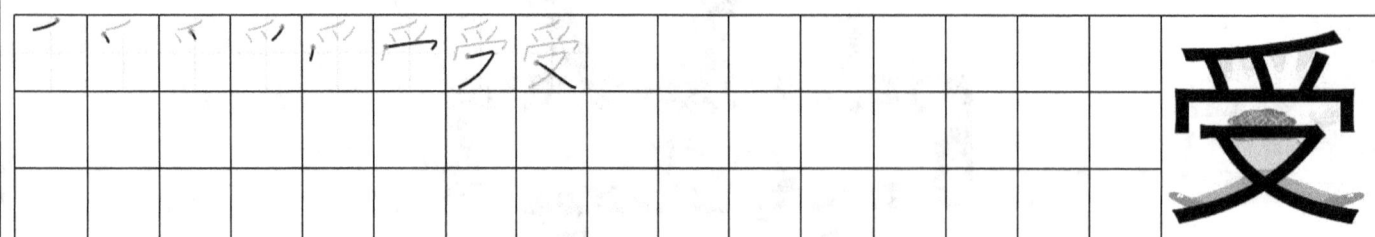

SIMILAR KANJI	Kun (う)	ODD (うけ)
愛 = Love 安 = Cheap	う 受ける = To receive, to undergo う と 受け取る = To receive	うけつけ 受付 = Receipt

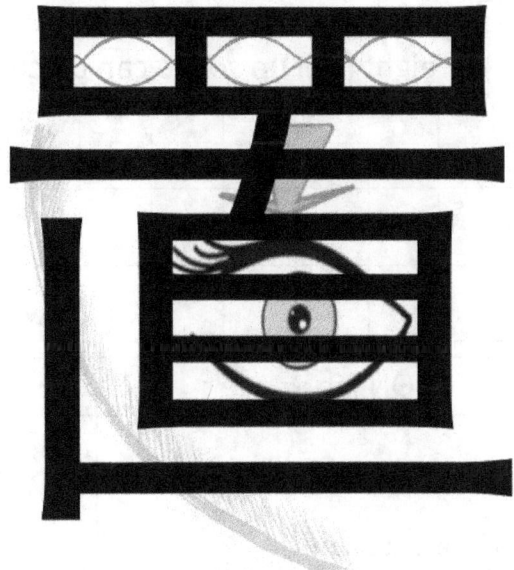

省 FOCUS, GOVERNMENT MINISTRY

"Very few (少) people know how to keep their eyes (目) focused (省)"

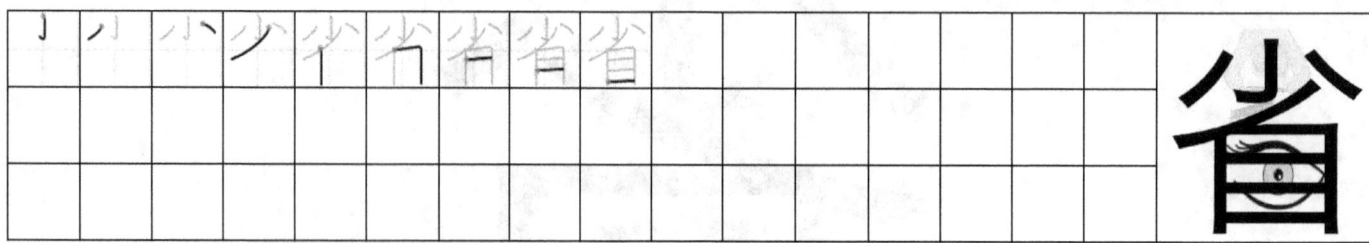

SIMILAR KANJI	Kun (はぶ)
少 = Few 劣 = Be inferior to	はぶ 省く = To omit, to eliminate

植 PLANT

"When you plant (植) a tree (木), you must place it straight (直) up"

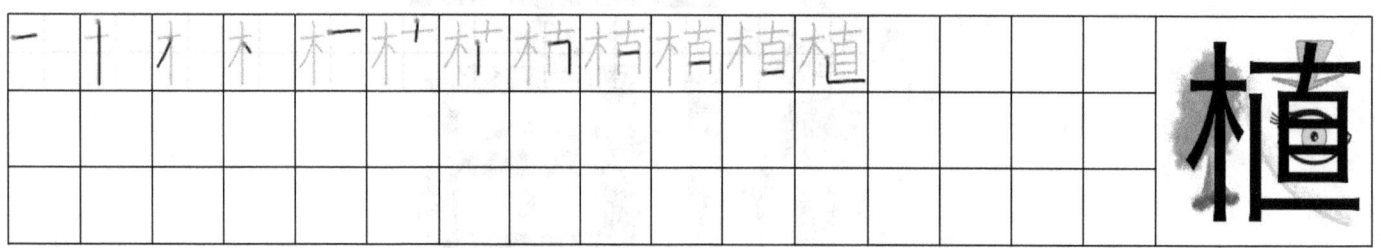

SIMILAR KANJI	ON (ショク)	Kun (う)
値 = Price 直 = Straight	しょくぶつ 植物 = Plant, vegetation	う 植える = To plant

置 PLACEMENT, PUT, LEAVE BEHIND

"Put (置) the net (罒) straight (直) up so we can catch anything that falls"

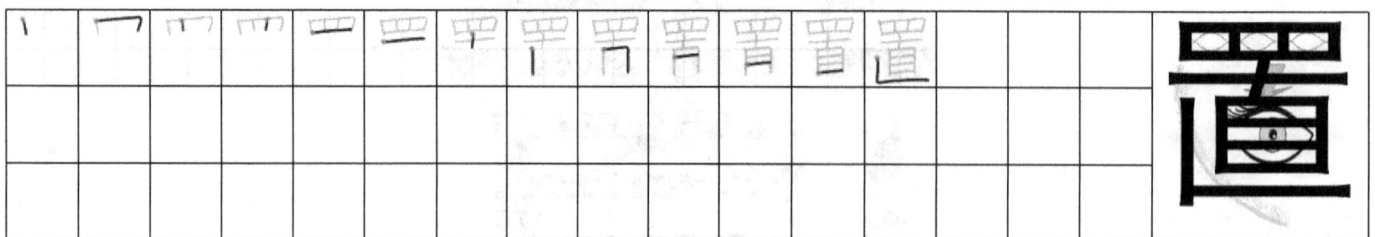

SIMILAR KANJI	ON (チ)	Kun (お)
買 = Buy 植 = Plant	そうち 装置 = Equipment, installation いち 位置 = Place, situation	お 置く = To put, to place

育

望

勝

育 BRING UP, RAISE

"Meat (月) has a good amount of protein that helps raise (育) children (云)"

SIMILAR KANJI	ON (イク)	Kun (そだ)
流 = Current 充 = Fill	たいいく 体育 = Physical education きょういく 教育 = Education	そだ 育つ = To be raised (child)

望 AMBITION, HOPE, DESIRE

"The king (王) hopes (望) his death (亡) is far away as the moon (月)"

SIMILAR KANJI	ON (ボウ)	Kun (のぞ)
聖 = Holy	しつぼう 失望 = Disappointment, despair きぼう 希望 = Hope, wish	のぞ 望み = Wish, desire のぞ 望む = To desire, to wish for

勝 VICTORY, WIN, EXCEL

"Use all your strength (力) to win (勝) the boat (舟) race"

SIMILAR KANJI	ON (ショウ)	Kun (か)
券 = Ticket 藤 = Wisteria	ゆうしょう 優勝 = Overall victory	か 勝つ = To win か 勝ち = Win, victory

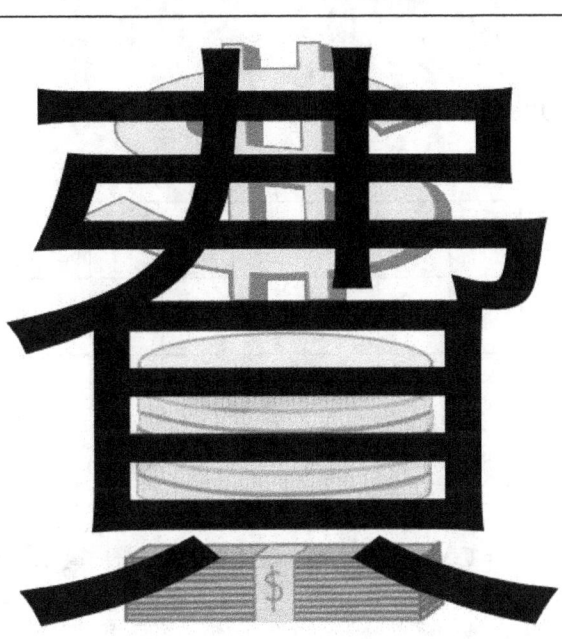

負 DEFEAT, ASSUME A RESPONSIBILITY

"The bent person (⺈) feels defeated (負) over all the money (貝) he lost"

SIMILAR KANJI
- 角 = Angle
- 貧 = Poor

Kun (ま)
- 負ける = To be defeated
- 負け = Defeat, loss

費 EXPENSE, SPEND, WASTE

"You've spent (費) so much money (貝) lately, even all the dollar (弗) currency you had saved up"

SIMILAR KANJI
- 賃 = Fare
- 責 = Blame

ON (ヒ)
- しょうひ 消費 = Consumption
- ひよう 費用 = Cost, expense

*Originally 弗 meant two arrows tied together. Yet, it is customarily used to mean "dollar" in Japanese due to the similarity with the dollar sign ($).

参 VISIT, GOING, COMING

"When I (ム) visit (参) my big (大) friend, I'm charmed by his bright (彡) personality"

SIMILAR KANJI
- 修 = Discipline
- 惨 = Disaster

ON (サン)
- さんか 参加 = Participation
- さんこう 参考 = Reference, consultation

Kun (まい)
- まい 参る = (Humble) to go, to come

*The original kanji 曑 was a person with three bright things on top. It gave the meaning to mingle.

練

続

結

練 PRACTICE, POLISH

"I'm headed to the east (東) to practice (練) my skills in yarn (糸) knitting"

SIMILAR KANJI	ON (レン)	
東 = East 凍 = Frozen	れんしゅう 練習する = To practice くんれん 訓練 = Practice, training	れんしゅう 練習 = Practice

*The original kanji was more about refining / polishing the yarns to soften them.

続 CONTINUE, SERIES

"He has to continue (続) selling (売) the yarn (糸) or he will be out of business"

SIMILAR KANJI	ON (ゾク)	Kun (つづ)	
売 = Sell 読 = Read	れんぞく 連続 = Continuation そうぞく 相続 = Succession	つづ 続ける = To continue つづ 続く = To continue	つづ 続き = Sequel

結 TIE, BIND, FASTEN

"Tie (結) your wish with a thread (糸) and place it in the good luck (吉) box"

SIMILAR KANJI	ON (ケツ)			Kun (むす)
詰 = Packed 誌 = Document	けっこう 結構 = Enough けっこん 結婚 = Marriage	けつろん 結論 = Conclusion けっきょく 結局 = After all	けっか 結果 = Result	むす 結ぶ = To tie

This book covers the 361 Kanji found in the Japanese Language Proficiency Test N3 and the main idea is to cover as much material as possible related to each Kanji.

If you wish to join me in this journey of learning Japanese, check out my social media! There you can ask questions and join our conversations!

@JLPTKanjiMnemonics

Also, if you have any suggestions or improvements for this book, feel free to e-mail me at:

jlptkanjimnemonics@gmail.com

ありがとうございます！

INDEX

あい	愛	154
あいじょう	愛情	154
あいする	愛する	154
あいて	相手	130
あげる	挙げる	236
あさい	浅い	172
あそび	遊び	250
あそぶ	遊ぶ	250
あたり	辺り	196
あたる	当たる	236
あつい	熱い	70
あびる	浴びる	232
あぶら	油	26
あらわす	表す	190
あん	案	216
あんき	暗記	40
あんてい	安定	262
あんない	案内	190, 216
い	胃	50
いいん	委員	272
いき	息	266
いし	石	66
いた	板	102
いち	位置	138, 280
いちばん	一番	220
いちょう	胃腸	50
いっしゅ	一種	74
いっしょうけんめい	一生懸命	144
いと	糸	90
いない	以内	190
いにん	委任	272
いのち	命	144
いはん	違反	194
いふく	衣服	104
いる	要る	264
いわ	岩	66
いわい	祝い	276
いわう	祝う	276
いんさつ	印刷	102, 266
いんしょう	印象	20, 102
うえる	植える	280
うけつけ	受付	244, 278
うけとる	受け取る	278
うける	受ける	278
うしなう	失う	260
うち	内	190
うつ	打つ	238
うつくしい	美しい	178
うま	馬	20
うめ	梅	28
うる	得る	270
え	絵	90
えいせい	衛星	58
えいよう	栄養	160, 264
えがお	笑顔	260
えらぶ	選ぶ	250
える	得る	270
えんじょ	援助	256
えんぴつ	鉛筆	96
おい	老い	42
おいつく	追い付く	244, 250
おいわい	お祝い	276
おう	王	36
おう	追う	250
おうきゅう	王宮	116
おうさま	王様	36, 204
おうじ	王子	36
おうだん	横断	192
おく	億	226
おく	置く	280
おさけ	お酒	26
おちる	落ちる	230
おっと	夫	36
おととし	一昨年	198
おび	帯	88
おべんとう	お弁当	236
おぼえる	覚える	254
おもて	表	190
およぎ	泳ぎ	232
およぐ	泳ぐ	232
おる	折る	238
おれる	折れる	238
おんだん	温暖	170
おんど	温度	170
か	課	206
がい	害	150
かい	貝	18
かいが	絵画	90
かいがん	海岸	68
かいけつ	解決	230
がいこう	外交	272
かいぜん	改善	248
かいだん	階段	120
かえす	返す	252
かえる	変える	168
かがく	化学	244
かがく	科学	122
かがみ	鏡	106
かかり	係	46
かぐ	家具	100
かくご	覚悟	254
かくじ	各自	210
かくじつ	確実	150
かくち	各地	210
かける	欠ける	140
かげん	加減	256
かこむ	囲む	200
かず	数	222
かぞえる	数える	222
かた	型	102
かたい	固い	240
かたち	形	146
かたな	刀	98
かためる	固める	240
かち	勝ち	282
かちょう	課長	206
かつ	勝つ	282
がっき	学期	198
かっき	活気	234
かつどう	活動	234
かつよう	活用	234
かてい	家庭	110
かど	角	106
かない	家内	190
かなしい	悲しい	168
かなしむ	悲しむ	168
かならず	必ず	168
かならずしも	必ずしも	168
かふん	花粉	74
かみ	神	128
かみのけ	髪の毛	54
かもく	科目	122
かもつ	貨物	94
かれら	彼等	182
かわ	皮	22
かんかく	感覚	156, 254
かんきゃく	観客	42, 130
かんけい	関係	46
かんこう	観光	130
かんさつ	観察	130, 262
かんじ	感じ	156
かんしゃ	感謝	156
かんじょう	勘定	262
かんじょう	感情	156
かんじる	感じる	156
かんしん	感心	156
かんしん	関心	150
かんする	関する	150
かんせい	完成	176, 268
かんぜん	完全	176, 182
かんたん	簡単	178
かんり	管理	94
かんりょう	完了	176
かんれん	関連	150, 252
きいろ	黄色	180
きいろい	黄色い	180
ぎいん	議員	206
きえる	消える	230
きおく	記憶	40
きおん	気温	170
きかい	器械	84
きかい	機械	84
ぎかい	議会	206
きかん	期間	198
きかん	機関	84, 150
きげん	機嫌	84
きこう	気候	76
きし	岸	68
きじ	記事	40
きしゃ	汽車	60
きしゃ	記者	40
きせつ	季節	74, 76
きたい	期待	198
ぎちょう	議長	206
きづく	気付く	244
きねん	記念	40, 156
きのう	昨日	198
きのう	機能	84
きのどく	気の毒	70
きふ	寄付	244

きぼう　希望 158, 282	げしゅく　下宿 116	さけ　酒 26
きまり　決まり 230	けしょう　化粧 244	さす　差す 136
きまる　決まる 230	けす　消す 230	さす　指す 54
きみ　君 42	けつえき　血液 54	ざせき　座席 88
きゃく　客 42	けっか　結果 28, 286	さつ　札 86
きゅう　球 82	けっかん　欠陥 140	さっきょく　作曲 254
きゅう　級 132	けっきょく　結局 114, 286	さべつ　差別 136
きゅうじょ　救助 256	けっこう　結構 286	さまざま　様々 204
きゅうそく　急速 176	けっこん　結婚 286	さます　覚ます 254
きゅうりょう　給料 132	けっしん　決心 230	さめる　覚める 254
きよう　器用 92	けっせき　欠席 88, 140	さら　皿 104
きょういく　教育 282	けってい　決定 230, 262	さんか　参加 256, 284
きょうかしょ　教科書 122	けってん　欠点 140, 222	さんこう　参考 284
きょうぎ　競技 276	けつろん　結論 286	ざんねん　残念 134, 156
きょうきゅう　供給 132	げんいん　原因 58	さんぽ　散歩 246
きょうそう　競争 236, 276	げんかん　玄関 150	さんぽする　散歩する 246
きょうちょう　強調 208	けんこう　健康 184	し　氏 138
きょうつう　共通 142	げんじつ　現実 150	し　詩 206
きょうどう　共同 142	げんしょう　現象 20	しあわせ　幸せ 160
きょうりょく　協力 146	けんぽう　憲法 216	しお　塩 30
きょく　局 114	けんり　権利 134	しかい　司会 38
きろく　記録 40, 214	こい　恋 154	しき　四季 74
ぎろん　議論 206	こううん　幸運 160	しき　式 136
きんこ　金庫 110	こうえん　公園 112, 118	じき　時期 198
ぐあい　具合 100	こうか　硬貨 94	じき　直 184
くうこう　空港 122	こうかん　交換 272	じきに　直に 184
ぐうぜん　偶然 214	こうくう　航空 242	しきゅう　支給 132
くさ　草 64	こうけい　光景 58	じさつ　自殺 278
くさき　草木 64	こうこく　広告 274	じじつ　事実 150
くだ　管 94	こうさい　交際 272	じしょ　辞書 254
ぐたい　具体 100	こうさてん　交差点 136, 222, 272	じしん　自身 52
くだもの　果物 28	こうそく　高速 176	しじん　詩人 206
くつう　苦痛 176	こうつう　交通 272	しずか　静か 174
くみ　組 132	こうばん　交番 220, 272	しぜん　自然 214
くみあい　組合 132	こうふく　幸福 128, 160	しそう　思想 154
くむ　組む 132	こうへい　公平 118	しそん　子孫 34
くも　雲 78	こうほ　候補 76	しだい　次第 220
くらい　位 138	こうむいん　公務員 118	しつぎょう　失業 260
くりかえす　繰り返す 252	こうよう　紅葉 64	じつげん　実現 150
くるしい　苦しい 176	こおり　氷 26	じっけん　実験 150
くるしむ　苦しむ 176	ごく　極 204	じっこう　実行 150
くろう　苦労 176, 256	こくばん　黒板 102	しっぱい　失敗 162, 260
くわえる　加える 256	こっせつ　骨折 238	しつぼう　失望 260, 282
くわわる　加わる 256	こづつみ　小包 248	じてん　辞典 212, 254
くん　君 42	こてい　湖底 60	じどう　児童 34
くん　訓 208	ことば　言葉 64	しどう　指導 54
ぐん　軍 44	こな　粉 74	しはい　支配 268
ぐん　郡 120	こまかい　細かい 180	しま　島 66
ぐんたい　軍隊 44	こむぎ　小麦 28	しゅう　州 122
くんれん　訓練 208, 286	こめ　米 30	じゆう　自由 138
け　毛 54	ころす　殺す 278	しゅうい　周囲 190, 200
けいかん　警官 46	こんやく　婚約 216	しゅくだい　宿題 116
けいき　景気 58	さ　差 136	しゅくはく　宿泊 116
けいこう　傾向 274	さいこう　最高 170	しゅしょう　首相 130
けいこく　警告 274	さいしゅう　最終 170	しゅっしん　出身 52
けいさつ　警察 262	さいしょ　最初 266	しゅっせき　出席 88
げいじゅつ　芸術 146	さいちゅう　最中 170	しゅよう　主要 264
けいと　毛糸 90	さいてい　最低 170	じゅよう　需要 264
けいやく　契約 216	さいのう　才能 166	しゅるい　種類 74, 142
けいゆ　経由 138	ざいりょう　材料 84	じゅん　順 142
けがわ　毛皮 22, 54	さいわい　幸い 160	じゅんちょう　順調 142, 208
けしき　景色 58	さか　坂 112	じゅんばん　順番 142, 220
けしごむ　消しゴム 230	さく　昨 198	しょう　章 210

しょう 賞	94	
しょうがい 障害	150	
じょうきゃく 乗客	42	
しょうきん 賞金	94	
じょうし 上司	38	
しょうじき 正直	184	
じょうたつ 上達	252	
じょうだん 冗談	208	
じょうとう 上等	182	
しょうにん 商人	242	
しょうばい 商売	242	
しょうひ 消費	230, 284	
しょうひん 商品	242	
しょうぼう 消防	230	
しょうわ 昭和	170	
しょくぶつ 植物	280	
じょしゅ 助手	256	
しょるい 書類	142	
しらべる 調べる	208	
しるし 印	102	
しんけい 神経	128	
しんこう 信仰	156	
しんごう 信号	156, 220	
しんこく 深刻	172	
しんさつ 診察	262	
じんじゃ 神社	128	
じんしゅ 人種	74	
しんじる 信じる	156	
しんそつ 新卒	40	
しんたい 身体	52	
しんちょう 身長	52	
しんぱい 心配	268	
しんまい 新米	30	
しんよう 信用	156	
しんらい 信頼	156	
じんるい 人類	142	
す 巣	22	
すいえい 水泳	232	
すう 数	222	
すうがく 数学	222	
すうじ 数字	222	
すくう 救う	246	
すし 寿司	38	
すばらしい 素晴らしい	270	
すべて 全て	182	
すみ 炭	68	
せいかつ 生活	234	
せいき 世紀	200	
せいきゅう 請求	260	
せいけつ 清潔	174	
せいこう 成功	158, 268	
せいじ 政治	46	
せいしき 正式	136	
せいじん 成人	268	
せいしん 精神	128	
せいせき 成績	268	
せいちょう 成長	268	
せいと 生徒	140	
せいふ 政府	110	
せいめい 生命	144	
せいり 整理	246	
せきたん 石炭	66, 68	
せきゆ 石油	26, 66	

せっきょくてき 積極的	144, 204, 226	
ぜったい 絶対	196	
せつやく 節約	76, 216	
ぜんいん 全員	182	
ぜんこく 全国	182	
せんしゅ 選手	250	
ぜんぜん 全然	214	
せんそう 戦争	136, 236	
せんたく 選択	250	
ぜんぶ 全部	120, 182	
ぞう 象	20	
ぞうか 増加	256	
そうこ 倉庫	116	
そうぞう 想像	154	
そうぞく 相続	130, 286	
そうだん 相談	130, 208	
そうち 装置	280	
そうとう 相当	130	
そうりだいじん 総理大臣	38	
そくど 速度	176	
そこ 底	200	
そだつ 育つ	282	
そつぎょう 卒業	40	
そのた その他	212	
そば 側	188	
そまつ 粗末	192	
たいいく 体育	282	
たいおん 体温	170	
たいしょう 対象	20, 196	
だいじょうぶ 大丈夫	36	
だいじん 大臣	38	
たいする 対する	196	
たいせん 対戦	136	
だいひょう 代表	190	
だいぶぶん 大部分	120	
たいへん 大変	168	
たいよう 太陽	62	
たいら 平ら	178	
たいりく 大陸	70	
たけ 竹	76	
たすける 助ける	256	
ただちに 直ちに	184	
たっする 達する	252	
たとえば 例えば	212	
たに 谷	118	
たにん 他人	212	
たね 種	74	
たば 束	90	
たま 玉	82	
たま 球	82	
たまねぎ 玉ネギ	82	
たんい 単位	138, 178	
たんご 単語	178	
たんじゅん 単純	178	
たんなる 単なる	178	
ち 血	54	
ちい 地位	138	
ちかてつ 地下鉄	78	
ちきゅう 地球	82	
ちへいせん 地平線	178	
ちゅうおう 中央	188	
ちょう 兆	226	
ちょう 腸	50	

ちょうさ 調査	208	
ちょうし 調子	208	
ちょきん 貯金	130	
ちょくせつ 直接	184	
ちょっけい 直径	224	
つうしん 通信	156	
つうちょう 通帳	88	
つぎ 次	196	
つきあい 付き合い	244	
つぎつぎ 次々	196	
つける 付ける	244	
つたえる 伝える	244	
つづき 続き	286	
つづく 続く	286	
つづける 続ける	286	
つつみ 包み	248	
つつむ 包む	248	
つの 角	*106*	
つめたい 冷たい	174	
つもる 積もる	226	
つゆ 梅雨	28	
つれ 連れ	252	
つれる 連れる	252	
ていあん 提案	216	
ていき 定期	198, 262	
ていねい 丁寧	124	
ていりゅうじょ 停留所	242	
てきとう 適当	236	
てちょう 手帳	88	
てつ 鉄	78	
てつだい 手伝い	244	
てってい 徹底	200	
てつどう 鉄道	78	
てら 寺	124	
てらす 照らす	268	
てる 照る	268	
てん 点	222	
てんけい 典型	102, 212	
てんこう 天候	76	
でんとう 伝統	244	
でんとう 電灯	104	
てんねん 天然	214	
でんぱ 電波	60	
と 戸	114	
とうあん 答案	216	
とうだい 灯台	104	
とうひょう 投票	86, 238	
どうぶつえん 動物園	112	
どうよう 同様	204	
どうろ 道路	118	
どく 毒	70	
とくい 得意	270	
とざん 登山	240	
とつぜん 突然	214	
となえる 唱える	270	
とばす 飛ばす	264	
とびだす 飛び出す	264	
とぶ 飛ぶ	264	
ともだち 友達	252	
ともに 共に	142	
とりあげる 取り上げる	278	
とりかえる 取り換える	278	
どりょく 努力	182	

とる 取る ... 278	はっぴょう 発表 ... 190	ふんいき 雰囲気 ... 200
とれる 取れる ... 278	はな 鼻 ... 52	ぶんか 文化 ... 244
ないよう 内容 ... 190	はなす 放す ... 248	ぶんしょう 文章 ... 210
なおす 直す ... 184	はなぢ 鼻血 ... 52	ぶんぽう 文法 ... 216
なおる 治る ... 46	はなみず 鼻水 ... 52	へい 兵 ... 44
なか 仲 ... 188	はね 羽根 ... 22	へいきん 平均 ... 178
ながす 流す ... 62	はぶく 省く ... 280	へいたい 兵隊 ... 44
なかま 仲間 ... 188	ばめん 場面 ... 106	へいわ 平和 ... 160
ながれ 流れ ... 62	はやい 速い ... 176	へや 部屋 ... 120
ながれる 流れる ... 62	はら 原 ... 58	へん 辺 ... 196
なく 泣く ... 234	はれ 晴れ ... 270	へんか 変化 ... 168, 244
なく 鳴く ... 274	はれる 晴れる ... 270	へんこう 変更 ... 168
なくす 無くす ... 214	はんい 範囲 ... 200	べんごし 弁護士 ... 36
なげる 投げる ... 238	ばんぐみ 番組 ... 132, 220	へんじ 返事 ... 252
なし 無し ... 214	はんけい 半径 ... 224	べんり 便利 ... 134
なっとく 納得 ... 270	はんこう 反抗 ... 194	ほう 法 ... 216
など 等 ... 182	ばんごう 番号 ... 220	ほうこう 方向 ... 274
なみ 波 ... 60	はんたい 反対 ... 194, 196	ほうこく 報告 ... 274
なる 成る ... 268	ひ 灯 ... 104	ほうせき 宝石 ... 66
なる 鳴る ... 274	ひえる 冷える ... 174	ほうそう 放送 ... 248
にがい 苦い ... 176	ひがい 被害 ... 150	ほうほう 方法 ... 216
にかいだて 二階建て ... 120	ひげき 悲劇 ... 168	ぼくちく 牧畜 ... 20
にがて 苦手 ... 176	ひこう 飛行 ... 264	ほし 星 ... 58
にっき 日記 ... 40	ひこうき 飛行機 ... 84, 264	ほそい 細い ... 180
にもつ 荷物 ... 92	ひこうじょう 飛行場 ... 264	ほほえむ 微笑む ... 260
にわ 庭 ... 110	びじゅつかん 美術館 ... 178	まいる 参る ... 284
にんぎょう 人形 ... 146	びじん 美人 ... 178	まがる 曲がる ... 254
ぬるい 温い ... 170	ひづけ 日付 ... 244	まけ 負け ... 284
ね 根 ... 72	ひっし 必死 ... 168	まける 負ける ... 284
ねがい 願い ... 210	ひつじ 羊 ... 18	まご 孫 ... 34
ねがう 願う ... 210	ひつよう 必要 ... 264	まじめ 真面目 ... 106
ねつ 熱 ... 70	ひてい 否定 ... 262	まだ 未だ ... 204
ねっしん 熱心 ... 70	ひとしい 等しい ... 182	まち 街 ... 112
ねったい 熱帯 ... 70, 88	びょう 秒 ... 192	まちかど 街角 ... 112
ねっちゅう 熱中 ... 70	ひょう 表 ... 190	まつ 末 ... 192
のうか 農家 ... 72	ひよう 費用 ... 284	まつ 松 ... 72
のうぎょう 農業 ... 72	ひょうが 氷河 ... 26	まっすぐ 真っ直ぐ ... 184
のうみん 農民 ... 72	ひょうげん 表現 ... 190	まつり 祭 ... 148
のこす 残す ... 134	びょうどう 平等 ... 178, 182	まめ 豆 ... 30
のこり 残り ... 134	ひょうめん 表面 ... 106	まもる 守る ... 262
のぞみ 望み ... 282	ひろう 拾う ... 234	まる 丸 ... 166
のぞむ 望む ... 282	ふうけい 風景 ... 58	まるい 丸い ... 166
のぼる 登る ... 240	ふうせん 風船 ... 92	まわり 周り ... 190
は 歯 ... 52	ふうふ 夫婦 ... 36	まんぞく 満足 ... 172
は 葉 ... 64	ふえ 笛 ... 96	まんねんひつ 万年筆 ... 96
ばい 倍 ... 224	ぶき 武器 ... 92	み 身 ... 52
ばいう 梅雨 ... 28	ふかい 深い ... 172	みずうみ 湖 ... 60
はいざら 灰皿 ... 104	ふくしょう 副賞 ... 38	みちる 満ちる ... 172
はいしゃ 歯医者 ... 52	ふくしょく 副食 ... 38	みどり 緑 ... 180
はいたつ 配達 ... 252, 268	ふこう 不幸 ... 160	みなと 港 ... 122
ばか 馬鹿 ... 20	ぶじ 無事 ... 214	みゃく 脈 ... 50
はがき 葉書 ... 64	ふし 節 ... 76	みゃくはく 脈拍 ... 50
はかせ 博士 ... 36, 40	ふしぎ 不思議 ... 206	みらい 未来 ... 204
はくぶつかん 博物館 ... 40	ふじゆう 不自由 ... 138	みる 観る ... 130
はこ 箱 ... 96	ふじん 夫人 ... 36	む 無 ... 214
はし 橋 ... 114	ぶちょう 部長 ... 120	むかい 向かい ... 274
はじめ 初め ... 266	ぶつ 打つ ... 238	むかう 向かう ... 274
はじめて 初めて ... 266	ふで 筆 ... 96	むかし 昔 ... 198
はしら 柱 ... 82	ふね 船 ... 92	むく 向く ... 274
はた 旗 ... 100	ふへい 不平 ... 178	むける 向ける ... 274
はたけ 畑 ... 68	ふまん 不満 ... 172	むこう 向こう ... 274
はつが 発芽 ... 64	ふり 不利 ... 134	むし 無視 ... 214
はったつ 発達 ... 252	ふるさと 古里 ... 124	むし 虫 ... 18

むしば　虫歯 18, 52	ゆ　湯 62	りく　陸 70
むじんとう　無人島 66	ゆうき　勇気 158	りこう　利口 134
むすこ　息子 266	ゆうしょう　優勝 282	りそう　理想 154
むすぶ　結ぶ 286	ゆうびんきょく　郵便局 114	りゅうこう　流行 62
むだ　無駄 214	ゆうべ　昨夜 198	りょう　量 148
め　芽 64	ゆうり　有利 134	りょうがえ　両替 224
めいじる　命じる 144	ゆかた　浴衣 *104*	りょうし　漁師 232
めいれい　命令 144	ゆき　雪 78	りょうしん　両親 224
めがね　眼鏡 *106*	ゆび　指 54	りょうほう　両方 224
めん　面 *106*	ゆびわ　指輪 54, 100	るす　留守 262
めんどう　面倒 *106*	ゆみ　弓 98	れい　例 212
もうしあげる　申し上げる 272	よい　良い 166	れい　礼 128
もうしこむ　申し込む 272	よう　様 204	れいぎ　礼儀 128
もうしわけ　申し訳 272	ようがん　溶岩 66	れいせい　冷静 174
もうす　申す 272	ようき　陽気 62	れいぞうこ　冷蔵庫 110, 174
もうふ　毛布 54	ようきゅう　要求 260	れいぼう　冷房 174
もくてき　目的 144	ようじ　幼児 34	れきし　歴史 194
もくひょう　目標 86	ようす　様子 204	れつ　列 134
もっとも　最も 170	ようするに　要するに 264	れっしゃ　列車 134
もとめる　求める 260	ようそ　要素 264	れんしゅう　練習 286
もよう　模様 204	ようてん　要点 222, 264	れんしゅうする　練習する ... 286
やく　役 140	よき　予期 148, 198	れんそう　連想 154, 252
やく　焼く 276	よこ　横 192	れんぞく　連続 252, 286
やく　約 216	よこぎる　横切る 192	ろうじん　老人 42
やくそく　約束 90	よさん　予算 148, 222	ろうどう　労働 256
やくにたつ　役に立つ 140	よそく　予測 148	ろんそう　論争 236
やくわり　役割 140	よてい　予定 148, 262	わ　輪 100
やける　焼ける 276	よほう　予報 148	わらい　笑い 260
やじるし　矢印 98	よやく　予約 148, 216	わらう　笑う 260
やど　宿 116	よろこび　喜び 240	わらべ　童 34
やね　屋根 72	よろこぶ　喜ぶ 240	
やめる　辞める 254	りえき　利益 134	

www.ingramcontent.com/pod-product-compliance
Lightning Source LLC
Chambersburg PA
CBHW051208290426
44109CB00021B/2380